It's Time to EAT

It's Time to EAT

EMBODY, AWAKEN & TRANSFORM OUR RELATIONSHIP WITH FOOD, BODY & SELF

Inge Sengelmann LCSW, SEP, RYT

ISBN: 1516886100
ISBN 13: 9781516886104
Library of Congress Control Number: 2015913245
CreateSpace Independent Publishing Platform
North Charleston, South Carolina

Table of Contents

INTRODUCTION

From Thinking to Being

I GREW UP THINKING. I was going to say, I grew up thinking that thinking was my identity, but I may as well stop at "I grew up thinking..." I certainly remember valuing thinking over feeling, and becoming excited when, in my teens, I first heard Descarte's assertion, "I think, therefore I am." I was my thoughts. What I thought, I was. I had no objectivity or distance from my thoughts. If I thought I was worthless, I *was* worthless. I drank at the altar of knowledge. I consumed information as if it provided oxygen and nutrients, not even questioning why I did it. It gave me a sense of self. I was a thinking, knowing being.

Nothing wrong with that, except that it's only a small part of a much bigger picture. I rejected emotions and sought to numb them, which in turn made them stronger and more unwieldy. I became a floating head, unaware of the information and resources my body sensations and human emotions held. My body became the object of my thinking, and what I thought about it was that it was too big and too uncomfortable. Of course, sensations and emotions live in the body, and mine were unnerving. So my floating head calculated calories, tallied up weights and clothing sizes, and mercilessly scrutinized photographs in an attempt to further disown and disconnect from those aspects of self which I found intolerable.

Body awareness is very different from body objectification, the tendency to experience one's body as an object to be evaluated for appearance rather than for function and effectiveness. In body objectification we are actually disconnected from our bodies, even if we spend hours thinking *about* our bodies. We are only concerned with the image of our bodies rather than with the actual subjective self-awareness of our bodies. Body obsession in eating disorder is a symptom of disembodiment, rather than of embodiment, and studies have demonstrated that low interoception – awareness of sensations experienced from the inside of the body and through the muscles, joints and skin – was correlated to higher rates of self-objectification as experienced by people with eating disorders. Embodied experience, with full interoceptive awareness, may actually reduce body objectification.

Personally, I used spirituality as a way to dissociate from bodily experience, rather than to connect to something greater from an embodied place. Ever since an experience of the nondual realm at age thirteen, I sought to escape the embodied life because I found it intolerable. I had no teacher to guide me, so meditation became a vehicle for escaping the world rather than being more effective in the world. I was engaging in a process that some have coined spiritual bypassing – the act of using spirituality to avoid dealing with our human experience with its inherent pains and traumas. It didn't work, so I contemplated suicide as a way out many times from the ages of fifteen to thirty. Thinking about dying granted me the relief of knowing that if my experience of life became unbearable, I could end it.

Eventually, as the only way to heal from an eating disorder and complex PTSD, I had to re-embody – from a shattered, fragmented self to a coherent self. My body gradually became an ally, the source of intuitive wisdom, the vehicle with which to process emotions, and further, an altar to the Divine. I became enamored with embodiment sciences and methodologies: yoga, chiropractic, acupuncture, craniosacral, massage, and various forms of body-oriented psychotherapy among others. Each of these modalities contributed, one by one, step by step, to my integration into a fully embodied individual whose soul, body and mind functioned coherently.

Only in the last couple of centuries has Western science begun questioning man's inner being, mental processes, motivations and potential. Thousands of years ago, on the other hand, experienced yogis developed an immense philosophy of mind and consciousness based on their internal explorations. These yogis established that the powers (or *shaktis*) inherent in the entire universe reside within us, and that the gateway to those experiences is our own body-mind with its various levels of perception. Today, more of the world is beginning to join the ancient yogis and the early pioneers of body psychotherapy. Somatic practices are becoming increasingly mainstream, and their effectiveness is being validated by neuroscience and social research.

Knowing my own experience of healing through the body, I rejoiced when I first read Antonio Damasio's *Descarte's Error*, in which he proposes a theory of "somatic markers" and stipulates that our reasoning stems from emotions, which themselves stem from sensory input from the body. We cannot reason, then, without emotional and sensory awareness. Or, we are reasoning, but because we do not understand what emotions and sensations are informing our behaviors, we are acting unconsciously. We are not fully conscious until these internal drivers of our behavior are illuminated by our awareness.

Recently I came across an article in the Buddhist magazine *Tricycle*. It featured an interview with embodied cognition philosopher Evan Thompson, who first published *The Embodied Mind: Cognitive Science and Human Experience* in 1992. The book was published in a second edition in 2015. My guess is that twenty-plus years ago the book was way ahead of its time. Apparently, we are now culturally more ready for its message. In the article, Thompson, who is a professor at the University of British Columbia in Vancouver, states that "cognition is a form of embodied action. Cognition is an expression of our bodily agency." Thinking that the mind is inside the head, he advocates, "is like saying that flight is inside the wings of a bird." Instead, he believes, "the mind is relational. It's a way of being in relation to the world. The mind exists at the level of embodied being in the world."

Allan Schore, author of *Affect Regulation and the Origin of the Self* and a pioneer in the neurobiological understanding of the impact of developmental trauma to the brain, has stated that in the 21st century therapy is naturally evolving to being a relational, experiential and right-brain process, rather than a talking, thinking, left brain process. Only in that way can we reach and repattern those implicit, pre-verbal states that are hardwired in individuals with early relational trauma. The brain is moldable, and with skill and guidance, new neural pathways can be wired. Mindfulness is one of the tools to help us achieve that, but only if it is mindfulness that is guided in a particularly skillful manner. Mindfulness alone is only the beginning, but mishandled it can simply reinforce the grooves that are already there.

The entire purpose of this book, and the goal of my candid self-disclosure, is to give hope. I pair memoir with reflections on research evidence and journaling questions for readers to provide a road-map for those who may be struggling through life with similar experiences. My story serves only to illustrate to both sufferers of eating disorders as well as practitioners in the field how embodiment- and attachment-based approaches can aid both in the understanding as well as in the healing of disordered eating. Most importantly, I want readers to understand that disordered eating patterns are simply a symptom of an underlying disorganization of the self, which we can reclaim through a process of embodiment. We judge what we do not understand. My attempt to bring to life new perspectives is to educate sufferers and practitioners about alternative and complementary treatments that could significantly alter outcomes.

Let me close with a quote from the interview with Evan Thompson. "Consciousness-in the sense of sentience, or felt awareness-is biological: consciousness is a life-regulation process of the whole body in which the brain is embedded. In the case of human consciousness, the context is also psychological and social. So even if we suppose that the brain is necessary for consciousness, it doesn't follow that consciousness is in the brain." So even as we tout "the new century of the brain," let us not forget the role of the body as both vehicle of experience and gateway to transformation.

CHAPTER 1

The Hunger Games: Dieting and Body Obsession are Making us Hungrier and Heavier

❧

At twenty-six, I stop consuming large quantities of alcohol on a daily basis and naturally begin to lose weight. Almost immediately, I become obsessed with "eating healthier." I choose salads and meats grilled to the consistency of shoe leather instead of packaged, processed or fatty foods. The eating disorder that had taken a supporting role position during the last years of my heavy drinking begins to emerge again, gaining prominence with every passing day. Soon, I am limiting more and more foods and becoming increasingly preoccupied with dropping weight. I begin to starve myself as a way to dissolve the body that I am in, with its fiery nerves and too tight skin, a body that betrays me daily with its uncontrollable sensations and cravings.

What begins as a desire to have a healthy diet mushrooms into full blown restriction within a few short months. My meals get smaller and smaller, starches disappear, sweets are forbidden, and fats of any type are a no-no. I get hungrier and hungrier, more and more anxious, and when occasionally I eat one string bean or rice kernel above what an internal dictator has allotted, it's an excuse to binge. And if I binge, I must purge. An eating disorder that began when I was thirteen and was temporarily dormant, or in partial remission, begins to emerge again, more furious than ever.

I'm ruled by the scale. It tells me that I deserve to be happy if I'm one pound or even ounces lighter, or sad if weight fluctuates upward. I weigh myself upon awakening, before the shower, after the shower, before a bowel movement, after a bowel movement, before a meal, after a meal. I calculate how much my clothing weighs by hopping on the scale naked, then clothed. All in all, I must weigh myself up to a dozen times a day, as if the number will be an indicator of my right to exist.

By Christmas, I am down ten pounds from the weight I was in February when I had my last drink, and I want to keep going despite the fact that I already look like a spider, all spindly arms and legs. I realistically catch a glimpse of myself at the gym one day, as I am lifting weights, and what I see is a skeletal figure, only to see it quickly morph into a plump woman with a fat rump and thighs made of cottage cheese. The fleeting image gone, I focus only on the fact that there is still a lot of flesh I want to eliminate until only sinew and bone remain.

But I am hungry, even though I will not admit it, even to myself. So on Christmas Day, I gobble up an entire, extra-large box of chocolates in one sitting – marzipan filled, nut filled, fruit filled. The entire assortment is gone and I cannot stop. Next stop: the porcelain bowl, a brownish, oily, slick sludge reminding me of my failure to curb my desires.

This binge sets off an intense cycle of starvation and purging, and by the beginning of February, I have lost twelve more pounds. I am at my lowest weight ever, and when I see the needle on the scale, I know I will not stop, and I know this is insane. A part of me wants to continue until there is nothing left of me. A wiser part is raising the alarm bells and urging me to get help soon. The space between those two urges is familiar. Ambivalence, confusion and indecision are central to my experience of life as far back as I can remember.

Pictures in my family photo album show a mellow, smiling baby, happiest when sitting on her father's shoulders. My mother looks withdrawn, thin, and has dark circles under her eyes. She admits to blaming me for her unhappiness.

"You were a terrible baby," she'll still say today, as a way to explain the situation.

My presence, my unending hunger, and my inability to settle, overwhelmed her and pushed her to reject me even more as my needs increased. By her own account, when she could not take it anymore, I was left alone in my crib to cry until my despair was extinguished and I collapsed. She recalls a day when she returned to my room after I finally got quiet, only to find me with my diapers off, smeared in my own poop.

I was consumed by my need for her. I was hungry for more nurturing, more cuddling, more tenderness, and more food – hungry with an endless, gnawing, insatiable hunger, and a hunger that wreaked havoc in my life and my relationships for years.

Even when I received nurturing feedback, I became unable to take in what was offered because it was accompanied with the same ambivalence I developed through my attachment with my mother. My biological impulse to attach had become intertwined with the fight-flight-freeze survival response to her depressed, angry state. As a result, I experienced chronic, low grade dissatisfaction and unwarranted self-pity for a large portion of my life. I felt alone and unloved even when those around me were present and emotionally available.

My unfulfilled hunger for connection was fertile ground for the development of an eating disorder that consumed me for many decades. The hunger to which I refer is clearly more than physical hunger, although certainly that is one dimension, and an important one. But it is more than that.

WHAT IS HUNGER?

Hunger: 1 a: craving or urgent need for food or a specific nutrient; b: an uneasy sensation occasioned by the lack of food; c: a weakened condition brought about by prolonged lack of food; 2 a: a strong desire; b: craving.

Hunger is a biological urge satisfied by the complex interactions between your physiological responses to food, your emotions before, during and after eating, and your thoughts about your body and self, all in conjunction with your evolving moods and desires as well as your actual nutritional needs.

I was born with an insatiable hunger, and it exhausted my mother's limits to such a point that it drove her to give up on ever being able to satisfy it. This dynamic of disrupted attachment trapped us in an endless cycle of mutual blame that lasted well into my adult life, when after much exploration and professional development I could finally understand what had happened. Understanding allowed me to release both my ingrained self-hatred as well as my self-righteous anger toward a woman who was only twenty years old when she bore me, the same age I was when I had my own child, and I know how unprepared I felt.

My mother relied on the parenting guides of the day, which advised new mothers to maintain rigid schedules with the infant rather than responding immediately to their distress cries. She admittedly blamed me for being a restless baby who could not be soothed despite her best attempts. I resented her for failing to attune to me in a way that I could trust and internalized the failure of our bond as my failure, which is a recipe for shame. She was angered by my inability to self-soothe, because I kept her up all night and tired her out until shadows encircled her eyes. I took the anger in and experienced fear, desperation and self-loathing.

I know this was not a conscious process, but a visceral, pre-cognitive experience that gets lodged as an automatic response in a person's nervous system. We know today, thanks to the work of brilliant scientists like Dr. Allan Schore, who explains that the self-organizing capacities of the developing brain happen in the context of the dyadic relationship with another human being.

Infants do not have fully developed nervous systems, and important neurological functions develop only through the attachment bond. It is through gazing into a loving caregiver's eyes and listening to them speak softly to us that we develop the parts of our brain that allow us to soothe ourselves. Until those parts of the brain are developed, we must rely squarely on others.

When those bonds are disrupted, impairments in emotional regulation develop, and patterns of dysregulation that lead to emotional and mental disorders later on in life get set in motion. If our caregivers "fail" us, or fail to be "good enough," we will project that imprint in most of our interactions. Even when a person's "look" is neutral, we might perceive it as threatening and react in the same way our infant selves did. The ancient sages were correct, we project our own reality out of our clouded consciousness, and very early trauma clouds it more than most experiences.

How can one heal, then, from these memories that are pre-verbal, pre-cognitive and pre-psychological? It's impossible, right? Fortunately for our era, the field has evolved and we are discovering that by exploring memories through the body, in present-moment awareness, we are able to uncover and renegotiate those bodily responses that were once buried deep in our unconscious. Most pre-verbal, pre-psychological experiences are integrated into our consciousness as implicit visceral responses that later become interpreted by the child's developing cognitive brain as thoughts and beliefs. It's why early attachment disruptions skew our perception of reality so that our distortions impair our ability to take in the good that is available once an imprint is made.

Whether the disrupted attachment bond caused me to be hyper-sensitive, or whether my highly sensitive temperament was genetically pre-determined is irrelevant. Scientists will continue to debate that for years. However, the new field of epigenetics tells us that environment activates genes that may otherwise not have expressed – and this starts with the intra-uterine environment.

If you've ever been accused of being "too sensitive" or have wondered why you feel intensely about experiences considered mundane by others, early attachment trauma may have initiated the cascade of hyper-response to perceived threats that may or may not be real. I know it did for me.

How does this relate to dysregulated eating behaviors and eating disorders? It's hardly a mystery. Although research into the role of attachment in eating disorder development needs to continue to explain the neural pathways, we know that eating disorders are more prevalent in adopted individuals, and many people with eating disorders exhibit avoidant, ambivalent or disorganized attachment styles.

We bond with our parents through holding, and most of that holding happens around feedings. Our first sense of self emerges from that body contact. We discover our contours, feel pleasurable sensations in our bodies, and know we exist. If the caregiver is not there, in the case of neglect, or if they are frightening or frightened, the sensations of fear and discomfort cause babies to disconnect from themselves. If left alone for long enough, a child will disown any sense of their body selves and ignore their most basic needs. Hunger, fullness and satiety cues become distorted or disavowed.

One of the visceral responses to high activation is nausea. This is why in states of high stress, children, and adults too, may vomit. Vomiting brings release and a sweet calm or numbness after-the-fact. In bulimia, this loop becomes conditioned and even the slightest activation – like a little too much food in the stomach, or a hurtful remark – will cause the response to re-occur.

While early attachment trauma may play a large role in the formation of these eating disorders, experts agree that these are complex disorders whose etiology remains largely unknown. They are multi-faceted and multi-dimensional in origin, presentation, and response to treatment. There are many theories of eating disorders, from the sociological to the neurobiological to the cultural and familial. Ultimately, each unique individual's phenomenological and psycho-physiological experience must be understood if it is to be addressed effectively and healed completely.

Reflections

A review of the literature indicates that individuals with eating disorders are more likely than others to have a history of trauma and, conversely, those with trauma are more likely to report disordered eating patterns – making trauma a risk factor for eating disorders. Any history of trauma is correlated with increased levels of impulsivity and dissociation, both of which increase symptom severity, longer length of illness, and poor prognosis

These rates may be higher when using a broader definition of trauma that includes any event perceived as life threatening that taxes the person's organismic capacity to protect their integrity. These may have been pre- and/or peri-natal events, or chronic patterns of threat such as abuse, neglect, and invalidation. Early histories of persons with eating disorders include injuries to the attachment system, without which the neural pathways that mediate affect regulation cannot develop. Because their pathways between limbic and cortical areas of the brain are undeveloped, they live in a constant flux of dysregulation and survival responses that eventually – because the sensations are intolerable - make a person 'numb' to most stimuli coming from the gut to the brain, including hunger and fullness signals.

Living in a world where bodily hunger is in constant conflict with the 'thin ideal,' keeps a person in a physiologically-stressed state of constant hyper-vigilance – and disconnection from internal body cues, as the focus on external markers of self-identity such as weight, clothes size and appearance become the focus.

Being 'fat' (or not unduly thin) in a 'thin world' oppresses young men and women every day. Trying to restrict food intake while flooded by a mass market of fast foods, deliberately manufactured to be addictive, and 'failing' leads people to feel 'betrayed' by their own bodies. When bodily responses fail to measure up to these impossible standards, eating disorders brew. And the diet industry is there to prey on those failures.

The 2014 U.S. weight loss industry was estimated to reach $60.5 billion in annual revenues for products and services such as diet soft drinks, artificial sweeteners, health clubs, commercial weight loss chains, OTC meal replacements and diet pills, diet websites & apps, medical programs for weight loss surgery, MDs, hospital/clinic programs, Rx diet drugs, low-calorie meals, diet books, and exercise.

Despite those staggering figures, there is little evidence that diets lead to long-term weight loss or health gains. Researchers from UCLA who conducted a rigorous review of studies on dieting found that up to two-thirds of all dieters who lose weight go on to regain it and even add more pounds. Many of those dieters go on to develop "pathological dieting" or disordered eating and a quarter of them move into full-blown eating disorders. Despite the clear evidence that restrictive diets as a form of weight control have been proven ineffective and unhealthy, dieting has become a cultural norm, and a large portion of eating disordered individuals receiving treatment report their eating disorder began as a diet gone awry.

According to a new movement called Health at Every Size, which proposes that weight and BMI are not valid markers for health, the "collateral damage" of this cultural obsession with dieting and thinness has resulted in a normative food and body preoccupation that plagues most men and women, hatred of self and body, eating disorders, weight discrimination and poor health.

We are currently living at war with our hungers. Even as large portions of the world's population are starving, people in wealthy industrialized nations are either eating to excess or furiously dieting to eliminate weight. Our insatiable appetites, our hunger for more of anything we think will give us happiness, and our relationship with food and weight have risen to the level of unsustainable obsessions.

Despite the billions spent on diet products and services, more than two-thirds of U.S. adults are overweight or obese. Others take their fear of weight gain to self-destructive extremes that morph into anorexia, bulimia, orthorexia, and self-harming extremes of exercising. To top it all off, weight loss does not always equate to good health.

So what are we really hungry for? Clearly, we are trying to feed our hungers with food, and it is not working. We eat and we eat and we eat and we are not satiated. Or we eat and we feel guilty and betrayed by bodies that will not conform to some culturally-imposed thin ideal, so we wage war on them, trying to beat, or surgically alter them, into some shape that has nothing to do with our biological make-up. Food is not satisfying us, and diets have failed to solve the problem. We must be missing the point. Hunger must have other dimensions we are ignoring, and so we are at war with our physical hunger, with food, with our bodies, and with our selves, as if they are the enemy. Beyond the fact that we may not be eating satisfying, wholesome, nutritious foods that will nourish all of our body's nutrient needs, we must be ignoring the other dimensions of hunger, such as emotional, mental or intellectual, interpersonal, and spiritual. These dimensions will be explored in subsequent chapters.

Journaling Exercises

Your unique story is important, and your understanding of what causes you to be at war with food or your body is unique to you. Fully understanding your experience will place you on the right track to begin your journey toward a meaningful process of transformation. You can rewrite the story, but first you must know the story that defines you at this time. Later in the book, you will learn some concepts and skills that may help you fill in the blanks and become free of that which keeps you at war with your needs.

1. What role did dieting and going hungry play in the development and maintenance of your disordered eating habits?

    ____
    ____
    ____
    ____
    ____

2. Who influenced your desire to diet? Was it a comment made by a family member, school administrator, medical professional, or peer? Or were you influenced by cultural messages in the media?

    ____
    ____
    ____
    ____
    ____

3. How has dieting changed your relationship to your body? Do you trust it more, or less?

    ____
    ____
    ____
    ____
    ____

4. How has dieting changed your self-perception? Do you like yourself more, or less?

    ____
    ____
    ____
    ____
    ____

5. Do you experience and give in to intense food cravings? Or do you engage in strict restrictive eating habits? Or both? When are you most vulnerable to the pattern?

____

____

____

____

____

6. What are some of the emotional experiences that may have contributed to the development of your current relationship with food and body?

____

____

____

____

____

7. What messages did you receive, and from whom, about your body and appearance? How did they make you feel?

____

____

____

____

____

8. What messages did you receive, and from whom, about your emotions? Were they validated or invalidated? Were they discussed and processed or were they ignored?

____

____

____

____

____

9. How content or discontent are you with the shape of your body and with your appearance?

____

____

____

____

____

10. When are you more content? When are you more discontent? What do you make of this pattern?

____

____

____

____

____

CHAPTER 2

What is Recovery, and do I want it?

THE FIRST TIME I HEARD the term *bulimia nervosa* I was a sophomore in college, recently married, and living in student housing reserved for married couples. I was watching a daytime television interview program featuring two women in shadow to protect their identity. By then, I had already been starving and purging for at least six years, especially viciously since I turned fifteen.

I was floored. This *thing* that I was doing with increasing frequency had a name, and they called it a disease, and they said it was treatable. In 1980, the idea that women starved and purged for a thinner body was still novel, and not too many people talked about it, much less called it a mental disorder.

When my husband came home, I welcomed him with:

"Hi honey, guess what? I have a disease called *bulimia nervosa*!"

He put away his knapsack and sat down to listen to me recount the history of this odd behavior that now had a name. Even then, rather than believing that he cared, I felt he was acting the part of a caring husband, just as I felt that I was acting the part of a wife intimately revealing her struggles. Later I would come to understand that my feelings of being an impostor playing a role were called depersonalization, an anomaly of self-awareness characterized by an experience of unreality in one's sense of self. This phenomenon can be experienced by anyone during incidents of high stress, but becomes a more chronic experience for those who have experienced severe trauma or a chronic, unrelenting stress response that doesn't abate.

"When I was twelve, I started to diet and fast to lose weight because I was uncomfortable with the size of my thighs and my growing curves," I told him.

He scratched his head, trying to understand why the size of my thighs was so important. Eating disorder beliefs, thoughts, urges and behaviors are incomprehensible to people who don't have an abnormal relationship to food, body and self. If they have any understanding at all, it is simplified to extreme attempts at "manipulation and control." The story is much more complex.

"How did you learn to purge?" He asked. "Isn't it gross to throw up?"

It would be to most people, I said, but to me it provided a way to not gain weight after bingeing. I did not like doing it, but I hated keeping food in even more, and I was terrified of weight gain.

"When I was thirteen, a friend of mine who was also trying to lose weight gave me a diet pill and told me that she purged by vomiting her food if she overate," I continued, recalling that day and the perplexing fact that we went on to eat all sorts of forbidden foods after taking the "appetite suppressant." Soon after that event, I was either dieting and fasting or bingeing and purging, depending on my level of desperation or degree of will power.

"Once I swam forty laps after fasting for three days then went home so famished and faint that I ate a stack of pancakes with butterscotch syrup and promptly threw it up," I told my husband on the day that I first disclosed to him, or to anyone, that I had a problem. "After I moved to the U.S. the problem escalated and I was purging secretly almost every night."

As I spoke, I noticed a familiar sense of shame increasing. I had been speaking to an empty room, without giving him much eye contact, but now I glanced furtively to assess his response to my growing disclosures. His face held an expression of concern, but it was not laced with pity or disgust, so I continued.

I described how the battle with my body raged with every new development – an increase in weight, wider hips, a thicker middle, and that disgusting flesh between my thighs. I told him how I never had a moment's peace from body-checking followed by harsh self-judgment. I explained that my appetite terrified me, and that I could not feed it to satisfaction and have the emaciated frame I craved.

I gave him the synopsis, the crib notes version of my experience with bulimia. I didn't tell him that I would eat an entire box of Krispy Kreme doughnuts plus a gallon of ice cream, or that I would sometimes purge in the tub while running the shower so my roommates would not hear me, how I avoided bingeing on foods that would not come up easily or might clog the drain. Oreos, for example, are a no-no. All that blackness is frightening because you don't know if you're throwing up blood.

On that night, I simply and naively told him, "Now that I know that what I do is dangerous, I will just stop."

Clueless about the insidious persistence of eating disorders, he accepted my claim.

"Okay," he said. "I hope so. I love you and I don't want you to hurt yourself."

And that was that.

The next day, I did it again and this remained a secret between us until I entered treatment eight years later at the age of twenty-seven, thinner even than the twelve-year-old who had started the cycle by starting a crazy diet found in a magazine in an attempt to straighten her nascent adolescent curves.

❧

At twenty-seven, I am one year clean and sober. Although I'm grateful to be sober, I don't like how I feel inside or how I look, and I feel generally discontent with my situation. I feel afraid most of the time – a sense of dread that lives like a hive of bees inside my core. I can't get rid of the discomfort buzzing underneath my skin. It's as if every nerve ending is electrified and won't be soothed. I personify the saying, "uncomfortable in your own skin." It's as if the suit is too tight. It doesn't fit. I want to claw at my skin to stop the itching, to rip off the too-tight feeling.

One day I do. After a fight with my husband, I run out the door in my sneakers, pounding the pavement to slam the rage boiling inside, scratching my forearms with my fingernails until burning red welts appear. Because I also bite my fingernails compulsively, I cannot do too much damage. I also hold back because I realize how crazy it is to take it out on myself. But at that moment, I do hate myself – I hate myself for feeling rage I cannot allow myself to express, and I hate myself for feeling trapped in an unbearably unhappy marriage. I know I've made a mess of things, and I do not know how to make the relationship work.

Prayer helps. Support groups help. But I want something to "take the edge off" and I don't have too many options. I still don't sleep well. While visiting my *abuela*, I think of stealing some of her Valium – *in case of an emergency*, I tell myself. I don't only because I've heard that popping pills is akin to "chewing your booze." It helps me to realize that even though I never had a pill problem, I could easily develop one.

I'm left with only one option – food. I crave foods that soothe, yet I am obsessed with dropping weight. Breakfast is a half-cup of citrus juice and half a banana because I've heard they balance electrolytes. Lunch is an apple and black or Cuban coffee. I eat lettuce and a small chicken thigh microwaved to a dry, tasteless, rubbery chunk for dinner. If I eat dinner at all. Vigorous exercise becomes a daily endeavor. But what I really want are Entenmann's crumb cakes, pastries, cheesecake and cookies.

The rush of hunger and the thrill of starvation gives me a way to disown, or dissolve, the body that I am in, with its electrical storm of discomfort. *If I get thin enough*, I think, *I can tolerate living in this world*. I'm not sure what this means, yet, but I will realize in the process of therapy that what I am trying to control or dissolve is not the world around me, but the uncontrollable sensations in my body that I am afraid will overwhelm me and kill me. My self-destruction, paradoxically, acts as a survival mechanism. I want to live, but I also want to escape, or flee the perceived threat to life that difficult encounters with others trigger in me. Welcome to the confusing world of post-traumatic stress syndrome, where bodily responses create a stark conflict with present-day reality, the body hijacked by some sensory trigger into a trauma vortex.

When my resolve to starve fails me, because I dare take one bite of that white chocolate chip and macadamia nut cookie at lunch and I am now making my way through a half-dozen bag, I lose control and binge rapidly on large quantities of food. I leave work, if I have to, and drive fast so I can get home to purge in private before my system can digest any calories. The compulsion is rabid.

A glimmer of sanity enters my mind one day, uninvited, and I decide that maybe I need help. And because my marriage also needs help, I ask my husband if we can see his therapist for couple's counseling.

Steve is a small man with a graying goatee, a veritable Freud "mini-me" who indeed espouses a psychoanalytic perspective of psychotherapy, delving into the depths of the subconscious for the cause of internal conflicts.

My husband and I show up together for the first session. I wear my smallest jeans, which for the first time are beginning to feel lose. I am conflicted about wearing them because, on the one hand I want to flaunt my bony figure, but on the other hand I want to hide it so I will not be labeled anorexic. I want to show off my arachnid arms, and I want to hide them because they make me look like a victim of a concentration camp. I feel sexy, and I also know – in my honest moments -- that I look like a flat-chested fifth-grader.

Steve talks to us about things that don't make any sense to me. Because I am hungry, I am also very angry. Full of rage would be a more accurate description of the energy bursting inside me.

I want to talk about how to save our marriage. Instead, he suggests that I eat.

"Eat some pizza," he advices. "I don't care what you eat, just eat."

He instructs my husband to monitor my bathroom use.

"After you eat, leave the door ajar if you go to the bathroom," he tells me, and to my husband, "Do not let her lock the door."

We agree, but I realize on day one that this just makes me angrier at him. I do not want someone to watch me go to the bathroom. I want my independence. I want to be left alone. And if I want to vomit, I don't want anyone to stop me. I cannot stand to keep food inside if it feels like toxic sludge slowly making its way to my thighs.

It's not that Steve did not know anything about treating an eating disorder. It's just that the psychodynamic approach did not work for me. Understanding that my vomiting may be symbolic of purging the primal rage I felt toward my mother did not help me to stop doing it – if it did, it would take many years to process that rage verbally, given that at the time I was not even aware of being full of rage.

"You don't need to protect your mother," the therapist would say to me. "She's not in the room."

I was only aware of being angry at myself – for not being perfect, for failing to measure up to what I perceived to be the high expectations of others, for believing myself to be unlovable and unable to internalize expressions of love when they came my way. But Steve had picked up on something. I could tell you I was not angry at my mother, but I resented her for rejecting any input I had regarding the care of my son while I was at work; for never having read any of the newspaper articles I wrote even after a few years of me working as a reporter; for criticizing how I dressed; and for looking at me with facial expressions that I deemed disdainful. My stories led him to the conclusion that if I wasn't angry at my mother, I should be.

It also did not help my marriage to put my husband in charge of whether I purged or not. It was unfair to put him in that position. He loved me, and he tried. He would massage my shoulders and coach me to take deep breaths when I sat down to my meager dinner of one measly chicken thigh, cooked to such a state of dryness that it measured less than two inches, and two or three broccoli florets. He would plead with me not to purge, and I would just yell at him to leave me alone.

I eventually get tired of the battle. My butt still feels too fleshy, but my seat bones get sore and bruised from sitting on aluminum bleachers when we go watch the local college team play baseball. And when the number on the scale hits eighty-eight, I know that even if I hit fifty-eight I will not be happy. I ask Steve if I can go to treatment. Frankly, I want to escape my life. I want someone else to fix my unhappiness. We begin to make arrangements for my admission at the only local eating disorder treatment center.

When I visit my parents to notify them, my father gasps in horror when he sees my shoulder blades sticking out of my workout gear (I am at the gym daily, sometimes for three hours).

"God, Inge, I can see every rib in your torso!" he exclaims with alarm.

I sigh in response. I am glad to be seen. I want everyone to know how overwhelmed I feel by life. Maybe if they notice how fragile I am, they will not expect anything from me. Maybe I have been starving for attention, even though I also want to disappear and avoid being noticed. I am confused by the unending series of conflicting impulses.

"I know," I reply. "I am going to go to treatment for anorexia and bulimia."

"To treatment?" My mother chimes in. "Why?"

"*Because*, I weigh eighty-eight pounds," I reply, unable to keep an edge of sarcasm from my voice. "Don't you think that is a little bit of a problem?"

She scoffs, "I once weighed eighty-seven pounds. I don't see what the problem is."

A low growl of rage and despair threatens to escape my throat, but I hold it in by clenching my teeth. When it's nothing but confetti, I curl up on my bed and sob a tsunami of dammed up tears. I sob until I'm spent and then I binge and purge "for old time's sake" before I pack my bags to go to treatment.

People don't understand my misery. Some, like my brother, admit it.

"I don't understand it, Inge. When I get too skinny, I just eat more, and when I gain too much weight, I just eat less. Why can't you do the same?" Peter tells me.

"That's the point, Peter," I say. "You are normal; I have an eating disorder."

I feel guilty for abandoning my seven-year-old because I feel selfishly incapable of operating in the world. I am consumed with a desire to disappear to avoid feeling the emotional pain that plagues me. My heart breaks for him, but I have shrunk so far into myself that I have nothing left to give. I am a shell of a person.

I spend only two weeks in treatment because insurance refuses to pay after I refuse to take antidepressants because I want to try to recover without dependence on drugs. I am afraid taking these drugs would violate my commitment to sobriety. I believe they are mood-altering substances, even though I am assured they are not addictive. As a result of my refusal, the insurance company assumes that if I'm not on meds, I do not need hospitalization. The fact that I am fantasizing about cutting my veins to bleed out the darkness is ignored, as is my sneaking in to exercise classes when I am not cleared medically, and my lack of any weight gain. Unable to pay cash, I am discharged into outpatient treatment with little more than a meal plan and instructions to return to a weekly support group.

ᘐ

The first year after my brief stint in eating disorder treatment, I engage in a highly restrictive "abstinence" plan endorsed by the treatment center, which views an eating disorder as an addiction to sugar and flour. I am unable to reconcile this model to my addiction to emptiness and my fear of food, but I like that it supports my urges to restrict entire food groups so I can maintain a low weight. I am barely able to go grocery shopping because I am overwhelmed by the massive amounts of food choices available, so I learn to go into the store and quickly grab the few familiar items I can tolerate before a blanket of terror engulfs me. I return to the car sweating cold and have to breathe deeply until my trembling ends and I can put the key in the ignition to drive home safely.

I continue to go to therapy with Steve, and I gain only four pounds in twelve months.

At the end of those twelve months, I get pregnant, and at eight weeks of gestation, I have a miscarriage. Was it due to being underweight and undernourished? Or was it due to the side effects of psychiatric medications I finally accepted taking? Or was it just fate? Or was God protecting me because divorce was lurking in my future? I will never know, and maybe it is irrelevant, but I am consumed by the guilt that I caused "her" death, my potential little girl that I was going to name Elizabeth Anne.

I spend two weeks in bed, trying to prevent the miscarriage, but the bleeding will not stop. It gets heavier and heavier and I worry that my body has expelled the fetus. Finally, the doctors inform me that they are unable to detect a heartbeat, and I must have a dilation and curettage, otherwise known as D&C, a procedure to literally scrape the contents of the uterus.

At the hospital, I cling to my desire for a different outcome as they ultrasound my belly, hoping against all hope that the faintest of heartbeats will emerge. I stare at the bean-sized shape on the monitor, pleading for it to be alive, grateful for the wait because maybe the doctors will realize they've made a mistake. Nothing happens. There is no movement, no heart beating.

After the surgery, I wake up to a colossal emptiness. It engulfs me so I can't breathe. Even the tears are dry, for now, and then the pain hits. It is immense, intolerable, entwined with remorse that I may have starved the fetus of nutrients or killed it (her, I am convinced, Elizabeth Anne, who will never be born) by causing an electrolyte imbalance with my vomiting. The physical pain can easily be managed with Tylenol. The emotional pain is impervious to all my praying, sharing, support from family and friends, or escape through binge reading and movies. I continue to diet and restrict, succumbing from time to time to the overwhelming hunger that leads to a binge, and the inevitable purge. Although these binge-purge cycles are less and less frequent, and I am eating three small meals a day, I am not free from obsession. Every meal is torture, as thoughts of weight gain flood me and I constrict against the life-force attempting to nourish me.

ꕥ

The correlation between my eating disorder symptoms and my difficulties with intimate attachments became evident during this period of pseudo-recovery.

Shortly after the miscarriage, I decided to end my marriage and met my second husband. Despite the red flags, I felt wanted and loved. I craved that feeling as much as I craved macadamia nut ice cream. They seemed to have the same effect on my experience. I quickly became inappropriately attached and dependent on this new man's approval for my emotional security. Because he disliked my quirky eating, I began to neglect what little recovery I had.

"You're such a pain in the ass," he would say when I requested that we eat at specific times or avoid restaurants where I could not find an "abstinent" meal. *He just wants me to be more flexible,* I would justify to avoid feeling invalidated and to ignore the abusiveness in his tone. I abandoned my meal plan and took more risks with food to gain his approval.

He also struggled with body image disturbances, overeating and over exercise. We began to indulge in certain foods together, sometimes eating a whole cheesecake between us, or a pint of ice cream apiece. We exercised two hours each day to keep our weight down. Despite the exercise, I gained some weight, but I did not mind as long as I had his approval. I eventually gained twenty pounds to reach what may very well be my biologically appropriate weight. I felt strong, but unhappy about my appearance.

Unfortunately, his approval was as elusive as his moods were volatile. The untreated bipolar disorder we did not know he suffered from caused him to change his tune on a dime. And when he rejected me, for no rational reason, I would despair and turn to food. Bingeing and purging in secrecy, sometimes multiple times a day when he was particularly violent, until I was left in a semi-psychotic state. Once, I even landed in a psychiatric hospital for two weeks and they would not release me unless I agreed to move out of his apartment. During one of our big fights, I picked up one cigarette to subdue my anger and began to smoke.

Our erratic and abusive relationship ended with a restraining order and finally in divorce when I was thirty-five. Another relationship led me to quit smoking, which in turn led me to gain fifteen pounds until I reached my lifetime maximum non-pregnant weight. It was gaining weight that led me to return to treatment because I had no peace. Every time I sat down to eat, the internal battle was exhausting. *Do I eat this, or do I not eat this? I feel so fat. I shouldn't eat anything. I need to lose ten pounds. Look at the size of your thighs! Feel the rolls on your stomach. Stop! Don't eat. But I'm hungry! You pig!* An endless dialogue between warring factions left me depleted from chronic tensing. I was not bingeing or purging more than once a month, but this partial recovery was too painful. I wanted more. I wanted peace of mind. I returned to more intensive therapy and support groups. Recovery was slow to unfold. But unfold it did, in its own time, at its own pace, until I was more motivated to recover, fully and completely, than I was to remain thin.

Reflections

"Being recovered is when the person can accept his or her natural body size and shape and no longer has a self-destructive relationship with food or exercise. When you are recovered, food and weight take a proper perspective in your life, and what you weigh is not more important than who you are; in fact, actual numbers are of little or no importance at all. When recovered, you will not compromise your health or betray your soul

to look a certain way, wear a certain size, or reach a certain number on the scale. When you are recovered, you do not use eating disorder behaviors to deal with, distract from, or cope with other problems." Carolyn Costin, MA, MEd, MFT

ൟ

This definition of recovery by leading eating disorder expert Carolyn Costin in her 2012 book *8 Keys to Recovery from an Eating Disorder* is the most comprehensive and satisfying that I have ever found.

In 1989, when I first entered treatment, I can't say that I wanted to recover. Yes, I wanted to stop bingeing and I wanted to stop purging. Those two behaviors caused me shame, and were more difficult to disguise because my eyes would get swollen, and I was developing blisters on the top of my hand where my teeth scraped the skin when I stuck my fingers down my throat.

Restriction, on the other hand, did not cause shame. It is ego-syntonic, I was told. It gave me a false sense of superiority and accomplishment. Paradoxically, I felt emotionally stronger (although physically weaker) when I was empty. I also wanted to wear a certain size (preferably zero), and maintain a certain number on the scale (less than ninety). Restriction and over exercise allowed me to achieve those eating disorder goals.

After treatment, limited as it was, I continued to eat the prescribed three meals a day, but they were composed of no more than a minimal amount protein, steamed vegetables to fill me up with as few calories as possible, and little or no starches or grains. I didn't gain any further weight and remained well under the minimum body weight the medical staff wanted me to reach.

The darkness deepened. Fantasies of suicide increased. I lay in bed staring at the ceiling, my mind traveling through a dark tunnel with no light at the end. The only pinprick of illumination was the fact that I had developed some faith in a spiritual reality, and the motivation to not leave a legacy of suicide to my son, who missed me and needed a healthy mom. I just couldn't seem to reach that ever-flickering light, in danger of being extinguished by the depression that enveloped me.

Long-term struggles with bulimia, anorexia and binge-eating are the norm. At least three dozen studies reveal that only forty-five percent of all bulimics experience full recovery even after years of treatment. Anorexia is the deadliest of all mental health disorders, having a high mortality rate due to heart failure or suicide. My experience was not the exception to the rule. I continued to struggle for quite a while with only minimal access to proper treatment.

I never stopped weighing myself, as it was recommended. If the scale inched upwards, I would complain to my friends that I was "too fat to live." This was only partially meant as a joke. I did feel an intense fear of living in a bigger body. I did not accept my natural body size and shape. I have short legs that are thin knees-to-ankles and much fleshier at the thighs. My hips are much wider than my thin (miniscule at the time) waist. Even at my thinnest, I still had buttocks that I considered disproportionate to the rest of me. My chest was flat and that did not bother me too much. The only thing I liked was how thin my arms were.

When the hunger got to me, or I was overwhelmed by strong emotions, I would give in to the urge to binge and inevitably purged. Binge foods became more limited in scope – white chocolate macadamia nut Häagen Dazs ice cream, tortellini with cheese sauce, or simply cereal with milk or yogurt and green grapes. The goal was to purge. There was almost no pleasure in eating. Purging provided a release that was quickly followed by a pleasant numbness that I equated to a heroine high. *I'm no different than a crack addict,* I would think as I lay on the cold tile floor. The frequency of the binges also gradually decreased to once a week, then once a month, but never completely until almost a decade later.

I did not know who I was, so I continued to have a self-destructive relationship with exercise for more than a decade, sometimes spending up to three hours at the gym desperately trying to change my genetics, and eventually running for hours to train for a marathon. I was definitely willing to compromise my health and betray my soul for the reward of remaining skeletally thin. Food and weight did not take a proper perspective until I was in my forties. They remained a primary concern and used up a large portion of my mental energy. As a result, my eating disorder morphed into various disguises.

Because I had been to treatment, and I attended support group meetings, I was considered to be "in recovery," such as it was. I was "abstinent" because I denied myself "binge foods," which encompassed just about anything tasty that scared me. The thinking at the time was that certain foods set off a compulsion to binge, but for me, the trigger was more mental and emotional. Eating pasta, for example, didn't make me want to eat more pasta. It terrified me to hold it in my stomach, and my mind drew a very real picture of my thighs expanding instantaneously. It was the cascade set off by these thoughts, images and sensations of panic that triggered the compulsion to purge.

This pattern of under-eating and over-exercising with periodic binge-purge episodes continued well into my thirties, and diminished only as I developed a more intimate relationship with myself through mindfulness and body awareness, and depended less and less on external relationships for my own self-regulation.

Gradually-increasing motivation to change led me to seek options outside the medical model of the day, and I started venturing into the "alternative" realm of approaches. I followed the guideposts that presented themselves along the way, such as information in an article, or a referral from a friend. I began to discern, using my growing inner awareness, what would be helpful and valid, and not just quackery and snake oil.

Journaling Exercises

1. How do you define recovery? Is it a broad or a limited definition?

2. How does your definition compare to Carolyn Costin's?

3. Do you believe full and complete recovery is possible? What would that look like for you?

4. Do you think believing you can recover can help you recover?

5. What motivates you to recover? What might increase your motivation?

6. Recovery is hard work. How willing are you to take the necessary actions to recover? What might these recovery actions look like in your case?

   ____

   ____

   ____

   ____

   ____

7. Are you willing to accept your biologically appropriate weight and shape and trust the wisdom of your body? Why or why not?

   ____

   ____

   ____

   ____

   ____

8. Are you willing to pursue flexible eating – honoring hunger, fullness, satiety cues -- and healthy movement for the sake of health rather than weight and shape?

   ____

   ____

   ____

   ____

   ____

9. What are the pressures you experience to recover?

   ____

   ____

   ____

   ____

   ____

10. What are the pressures you experience that impede your recovery?

____

____

____

____

____

CHAPTER 3

The Disembodiment Epidemic: The Role of Disconnection in Disorders

❧

At thirteen, when my body developed its curves and my pants accentuated the slope of my buttocks, I began to get looks. I remember not wanting the lecherous man at the grocery store to stare at me as I walked by. I remember sensing the impertinent ogling piercing my backside, turning around and returning the glare, then scrambling away in shame, wanting to hide and never wear those pants again. For years, I would engage in a battle to reduce the size of my (shameful) butt to avoid being looked at without my permission, while at the same time craving attention because to be wanted meant security (a.k.a. survival).

I never wore a bathing suit without a cover when I walked around. Sunbathing was a favorite pastime – bronzed skin being considered attractive by my peers. I could lay on a towel or lounge chair in my bikini, but the minute I had to get up I wrapped a towel around my middle, or put on a T-shirt that went down to my knees. In my early teens I even wore a T-shirt to swim.

"Why do you have to wear a T-shirt?" An older boy asked, as his hand reached out to lift the T-shirt. My reaction was swift, quickly pulling the T-shirt back down over my midriff, a quiver of shame flashing through me in a nanosecond – shame to be seen, and shame that I needed to hide, which obviously was considered 'weird' by my same-aged peers.

Memories of my high school years are a blur, a string of hazy events emerging out of the fog of dissociation and intoxication that makes them blend one into the other. The few memories I recall, I try to make vivid for you by pasting together fragments like a connect-the-dots puzzle or paint-by-numbers picture. In my mind, there is a shimmering mirage quality to the images because, as addictions and eating disorders erupted, the sharp edges of my experience were obscured.

During this period, the disordered eating habits that had emerged in pre-pubescence increased, and my unhappiness grew into a pervasive misery that muddied the waters of my sentient capacity. I seemed to oscillate between the crippling numbness of disconnection and an unbearable discomfort when I experienced the sensations that inhabited my body. When I felt my body at all, what I noticed was the rubbing flesh between my thighs and I wanted to obliterate it.

Given my insatiable psychological appetite for more, and the physical cravings fueled by the marijuana I smoked with increasing frequency, my weight had increased steadily after I moved to New Orleans at the age of fourteen and without my family, who remained in war-torn Nicaragua. There, an abundance of food was available to feed my temptations and soothe my preoccupations. The endless candy bars at the local drugstore, the pecan waffles at Magnolia Grill, the peanut butter cups and candied yams in the school cafeteria – they beckoned with their novelty. I was well fed physically, yet rarely felt nourished emotionally.

The first summer back in Nicaragua came after four months of steady weight gain in New Orleans. The numbers are irrelevant, but suffice it to say that I was now in a more rounded and fleshy body – an evolving woman's body with curves and breasts that was a far cry from the emaciated child's figure that arrived in February. It's not that I did not want breasts (although I did not want breasts like my mother's, enhanced by silicon when I was eight years old), but I did not want the wide hips and rounded bottom that went along with them. On a five-foot frame, a weight gain of about ten pounds felt enormous. I had now crossed the dreaded hundred-pound mark, and more was yet to come.

"God, Inge!" My brother exclaimed when he first saw me after my return. "Your thighs are huge!"

My horror was palpable.

"I need to go on a diet, immediately, so I can fit into my old bikinis," I thought, the thought fueling an urge that bordered on compulsion.

And so I did. The diet consisted of daily doses of Ritalin, easily purchased without a prescription, a slice of homemade wheat grain bread, plus a half-cup of plain yogurt with a teaspoon of honey at every meal. I did not deviate for at least two months and soon I had dropped to nearly ninety pounds. The Ritalin was delivered by the pharmacy by a messenger on motorcycle, and I paid the fifteen *córdobas* or so per box (about two dollars in those days).

Stimulated by the methylphenidates, I went out every night and did not pass on the wine, which soon gave me acid heartburn on a regular basis and made me want to eat even less. I was obsessed with the number on the scale – getting on before breakfast, after breakfast, before shower, after shower, with clothes, without clothes, and on and on. Anything above ninety-two meant limiting my intake even more for that day. Did I continue to drink and smoke pot? Of course. Do I remember much about that summer other than my strict regimen? Not much.

I truly don't recall much about my interactions with my parents (who seemed too busy to notice my behavior), or what was going on in my country (then in the throes of a violent revolution), much less the details of my friends' lives (going through their own adolescent growing pains). My attention was narrowly focused on obtaining the Ritalin, religiously preparing my very small and limited meals, hopping on the scale to keep track of the weight loss, the lack of satisfaction I felt when I leveled off just above ninety pounds, and the lengths I went to every week to make sure that Liska and I could get rides to parties where we could drink and smoke pot. You could say all this is typical behavior for a teenager, but I know teenagers who are much less self-centered and don't have the personality traits of a self-centered addict-in-the-making.

In the self-centeredness of self-starvation, no one else exists other than your hunger and your obsession to drop even more weight.

After weeks of food deprivation, we return to Louisiana just days before my fifteenth birthday, which falls right on Labor Day. Aunt Irma's lover takes us to Biloxi, Mississippi for the holiday festivities. I am homesick and depressed by the fact that I will turn fifteen away from my family, a family I don't want to live with but I can't stand to be apart from. I am torn, more and more, by conflicting impulses to connect with them while simultaneously push away from them – both a sign of normative adolescent individuation but compounded by the after-effects of disorganized attachment from early life trauma. I am desperately anxious and lonely when I am apart, but as soon as I approach, an intolerable fear and disgust bubbles up to the surface.

This is my first birthday away from home. My mother has given me her diamond engagement ring as a present to celebrate this milestone in my life and to emphasize our connection, but it doesn't seem to cut it for me. Maybe I am just ungrateful and cannot appreciate her gesture because I so automatically reject her, or maybe I am deeply aware that a material object cannot satisfy the inner need that I feel that never seems to feel satisfied. Whichever it is, I feel a gnawing emptiness and a grief that feels stuck just below my collarbone.

Families are flocking to the beach. Barbecues are fired up. Hot dogs are on the grill. American flags are waved by everyone, and near nightfall, sparklers are handed out to all as we get ready for the fireworks. I slowly walk away, aware that I am allowing myself to be shrouded in self-pity but not caring. I want to nurse it like a newborn baby. I look at the ring as I withdraw from the crowds and cry, crocodile tears at first, then something more genuine follows. These are the thoughts that pester my mind: I don't like American celebrations with hot dog barbecues and Lays potato chips. I don't feel special to Irma and Dick, even though they brought us here to celebrate and the evidence is that they care about me. I believe Liska cares, but nothing she says or does seems to cheer me up. I feel like the Pigpen character in Charlie Brown, walking around with a dark cloud over my head that weighs me down and sucks the air out of my atmosphere.

We go to our rooms and order several slices of cheesecake. I could eat cheesecake all night long and still not be satisfied despite the deliciously sweet and milky taste and texture of the food. My taste buds are temporarily happy, but the feeling of expansion in my thighs is immediate and panic sets in. I feel disgusted that I have now broken my pattern of starvation. I imagine that soon, fifteen pounds will return to weigh me down. The heaviness matches my mood, which is plummeting like sinking lead. Although I have purged before, when I do it on this night, I know that this is my new friend. My bond to this behavior is fixed, and it will take more than two decades to untangle. It is driven by a profound disconnection from my self – my body self, my emotional self, my authentic self. I know how to objectify my body, but not how to recognize its needs, much less its messages.

❧

The level of disconnection in which I lived first dawns on me at age twenty-eight. I am with a group of friends at a restaurant after an all-day spiritual workshop. It is a classic diner with bright lights and a metallic salad bar station in the middle. I stare at the items encased in ice as Brian, the workshop leader, approaches me and asks, "Aren't you hungry?"

I startle and gaze at him wide-eyed, sunken cheeks making my eyes look much bigger than they are.

"No, not really," I answer. "I don't have much of an appetite lately."

"Inge, when's the last time you ate?" he insists.

I have to think about it and count back to early that morning. It has been at least nine hours. I want to lie to him, but I can't. We just spent all day talking about spiritual principles, starting with honesty. Besides, I trust him. He's a nice and gentle man who is not afraid to wear pink socks.

"Nine hours," I whisper, looking down at the cold tiles on the floor.

He sighs, and makes a suggestion: "Why don't you ask your body if it's hungry or not?"

I've never thought of asking my body anything, much less if it's hungry. My head decides everything. Thinking predominates, even if it's distorted and deluded. Decisions about my body are made based on external ideas, such as a number on a scale, or the size of my jeans (zero by this time). Emotional and physiological needs are not on my radar, even though lack of food has caused me to become more rigid, obsessive and nervous. Spirit resides far above the crown of my head, a place I seek as an escape from being embodied and alive. Meditation as dissociation, and prayers to die in my sleep -- that was my spirituality in the 1980s.

I look up and see his kind eyes, shudder, and quickly look down again, embarrassed, overwhelmed by the intimacy of being seen exactly as I am: hungry. My craving for nourishment and nurturing shame me. I would rather die than acknowledge it, much less experience the pleasure of filling my plate and delighting in the tastes food has to offer.

"I guess I am hungry." I am surprised to recognize the pangs of an empty gut. I allow myself a small plate of salad with cottage cheese and raw vegetables. I eat it with greed, and shame, and gratitude, and guilty delight, all rolled into a big emotional crêpe.

I begin to acknowledge that perhaps there is a body connected to my head, linked by my fragile neck -- a body with needs, desires, information, maybe even wisdom (although it will be a while before my body's wisdom arises and makes itself known to my brain's conscious awareness).

Reflections

Dissociation from bodily experience, leading to a chronic disregard of the body's needs that reinforces the experiential avoidance, is a hallmark of these disorders regardless of where they fall on the spectrum – starvation and emaciation in anorexia, binge-purge cycles in bulimia, or binge eating and obesity in the other extreme. Paradoxically, the war is waged in the body as seemingly self-destructive behaviors are used to eradicate, manage or soothe emotions and sensations perceived as undesirable and even dangerous.

Studies of brain functioning in individuals with anorexia and bulimia also have shown impairments in the functioning of the insula and the anterior cingulate gyrus, areas responsible for interoceptive awareness, the integration of sensory information and emotions, the regulation of aggressive impulses, as well as behavioral motivation and coordination of motor impulses.

The insula is also responsible for assigning reward value to foods, a function disrupted in persons with anorexia who respond differently to taste stimuli. Furthermore, these same areas of the brain are largely responsible for the perception of the body-in-space and when impaired lead to symptoms of body dysmorphia, at worst, or body dissatisfaction, at best.

In bulimia, food serves to soothe sympathetic over-activation but because satiety responses have been interrupted a binge occurs, leading to a purging discharge that serves to expel uncomfortable sensations from the body. Once purged, the person experiences the numbness characteristic of a dorsal vagal response. Because there is evidence of a destabilization of the vago-vagal feedback loop in bulimics, relapse is common and beyond the locus of control of the sufferer once the binge-purge cycle becomes 'hard-wired'. This requires a titration of the nutritional re-education phase within the client's window of tolerance to try feared foods and tolerate fullness. In my experience, my bulimic patients have the highest states of hyper-arousal and require significant assistance to develop somatic grounding, orienting, and settling skills before they can be helped to discharge the activation they experience, which is usually expelled through vomiting or laxatives until other skills are developed.

Overweight/obese compulsive overeaters and binge eaters, on the other hand, display similar shutdown or disconnection from internal states as anorexics. Anorexics become significantly aroused by the feeling of food in the stomach, while overeaters are triggered by the sense of emptiness and hunger – even if at a more subconscious or autonomic body level. These groups require help in increasing awareness of arousal states through skills in tracking bodily sensations mindfully so these arousal states can be safely discharged and not induce either starving/dieting or overeating behaviors.

People often ask themselves, how can a person with an eating disorder claim to be disconnected from their bodies when they are constantly obsessed with their bodies? There is a difference between body awareness and objectification of the body. Body awareness refers to the concept of interoception, which is the perception of body sensations as they relate to physical cues or emotional cues that inform and form our internal sense of self. Body objectification refers to an obsession with the body as an object to be controlled and shaped, and can happen when person's sense of self, beyond how we appear to others, is absent, fragmented or underdeveloped. Interoception can build self-awareness and reduce the need for external validation.

Journaling Exercises

1. What is the state of your relationship to your body? Do you love it or hate it? Do you listen to it or invalidate its messages? (e.g. needing to rest but drinking more coffee to keep going; ignoring hunger because you are focused on an external goal to fit into smaller jeans; eating beyond fullness because you do are not aware of sensations or emotions)

   ____

   ____

   ____

   ____

   ____

2. How connected are you to your body's sensations, including but not limited to sensations of hunger and fullness?

____
____
____
____
____

3. How often do you pay attention to what is happening in your body, e.g. noticing if your breath is fluid or constricted, your heartbeat fast or slow, or your muscles relaxed or tense?

____
____
____
____
____

4. How aware are you of your emotional needs? Are you aware of physical sensations that may alert you to the nature of the emotion you are feeling?

____
____
____
____
____

5. List the needs you are meeting.

____
____
____
____
____

6. List the needs you are ignoring.

____

____

____

____

____

7. How do you view yourself? What qualities in yourself do you value beyond appearance?

____

____

____

____

____

8. How do others view you? What qualities in yourself do they value in you, beyond appearance?

____

____

____

____

____

9. How do you connect to your experience? How do you disconnect?

____

____

____

____

____

10. How do you feel when you connect with your experience? Do you have judgments or evaluations (good vs. bad) about it? What if you just noticed without judging?

____

____

____

____

____

CHAPTER 4

Embodiment to Restore Wellness: The Role of Connection in Healing

"…the experience of one's self in the world as a cognizant being does not solely emerge from neural activity within the brain. Instead, it involves a complex interplay of brain, body and environment, and the seamless integration of interoceptive, proprioceptive (including vestibular), kinesthetic, tactile, and spatial information" (Schmalzl, Crane-Goudreau & Payne, April 2014 in Frontiers of Human Neuroscience)

At the same time that my second marriage was dissolving, my failure to overcome anxiety and depression made me open to new ideas. I was willing to try anything to heal from the negative impact of chronic stress in my life. The medical model had failed me. Medications and psychiatric treatment kept me trapped in a loop of ever-increasing helplessness.

By 1995, I had been on numerous antidepressants – tricyclic, serotonin-reuptake-inhibitors (SSRIs), of which Prozac was the best known, and finally serotonin-norepinephrine-reuptake-inhibitors (SNRIs), with Effexor topping the list. The latest failure had been Luvox, an SSRI marketed as an obsessive-compulsive-disorder (OCD) drug that caused me intense nervous agitation. Fortunately, I refused the anxiolytics (anti-anxiety) offered by every doctor I saw. I had enough insight to know that I would have to stop consuming massive amounts of caffeine -- Iced Venti Americano with four shots of espresso twice a day -- before conceding that my anxiety was not caused by caffeine toxicity and would be best treated with drugs, and not with breathing, meditation or exercise.

Spirituality, as I experienced it then, had only taken me so far. It kept me from killing myself and holding on to hope that a benign, creative force in the universe would guide me to freedom from suffering. But I was seeking freedom from suffering by disconnecting from life. In other words, spirituality was something ethereal and above my intellectual head. There were no tethers to pull me down into my body, the earth, and life in general. I sought spirituality for the purposes of dissociation. I wanted a spiritual bypass rather than skills and strength to deal with life on life's terms.

I did not understand that non-duality meant that everything in the manifest realm of existence *was* spiritual, that nothing that exists in creation is separate from Creator (whomever, or whatever that might be). I wanted to be taken out of *here*, and brought *somewhere else* where I would experience *only* bliss. I kept thinking there was something wrong with me that bliss was not the constant state of my being. I didn't know how to navigate the ups and downs of life.

"I can't meditate," I would tell myself and others. When I sat and observed the contents of my mind, the state of my breath, and the landscape of my body, it was hell. My thoughts were like a wild horse when it has lost control, and there is no pulling of the reins to make it stop. My breath was in a constant state of constriction which meant that I rarely exhaled and my carbon dioxide levels were probably very low, putting my biochemistry in crisis and therefore affecting my moods. My emotions were one big black hole of fear and pain that consumed everything in its path. And my body felt like a jittery mass of tension and distress. Who would want to meditate if this is what they will encounter? And yet, in time, I would come to know that the only way out is through. I had to learn to sit with what was, so I could access true, non-addictive bliss. When I learned to do that, darkness dissolved and light pervaded.

Since I started abstaining from mood-altering substances in 1988, and until 1995, I had grown spiritually. However, I wasn't yet embodying that spirituality. What I had learned in those seven years was to seek, to become a spiritual explorer. Yes, I was a seeker of blissful experiences in order to soothe my emotional pain; *and* I was also a seeker of Truth, with a capital T. When you seek, with an open mind, a willing heart and an implacable spirit, you can't help but find. And as you find, you seek more, because the more you know, the more you realize you don't know. At seventeen, I thought I knew everything and no one could guide me; at twenty-seven, I realized I knew nothing and needed to be guided daily; by the time I reached thirty-seven, I was beginning to get the hang of the drill.

For years, my spirituality had consisted of prayers learned from books, reading and studying ancient spiritual texts with metaphysical teachers, reading spiritual books by more contemporary authors such as *The Practice of the Presence of God* by Brother Lawrence, and *Sermon on the Mount* by Emmet Fox. I read books and attended meditation meetings. I prayed in gratitude and in desperation. I prayed to have my most glaring shortcomings removed. I prayed for protection. I prayed for serenity when there was none. I prayed in my head and it had a soothing effect on my body and my emotions, so I continued to pray. "God could and would if He were sought," I was told. I decided that whether or not God existed was irrelevant. Prayer was helpful. It changed the way I was thinking, and therefore it changed the landscape of my emotions. I am sure it also helped me to breathe better, but I did not have an acute sensitivity to anything but a global sense of improvement from acute distress to normative distress, rarely bliss.

In late 1995, my seeking led to my first experience of bodywork in the form of a network chiropractor named Paul. This was the beginning of an exploration that freed me from the effects of stress and trauma and eventually led me to work as a somatic psychotherapist.

But on the first day, I was not sure that I liked it.

I arrived on a weekday afternoon at the clinic owned by Paul and his sister, Charlene. After filling out some paperwork, I was led into a room with multiple massage tables. This was the first surprise. Whatever they were going to do to me would be done in a public setting, with other people around. I may have expressed my concern, because they led me to one of their private rooms.

The practitioner came in and lightly touched different areas of my spine – no wild manipulations, no cracking of my vertebrae, just lightly tapping and prodding with one or two fingers. My doubtful and impatient mind went to work. "What is this? This is not doing anything." Of course, I was fairly numb and disconnected from bodily experiences, used to awareness of mental formations and not much sensory information or emotional intelligence. While I could name "anxiety" and "depression" as causing me misery, I could not label nor identify their corresponding physiology. They were mere concepts to encapsulate global unhappiness.

As the session went on, I began to sense some movement of energy along the spine that caused me pain. The pain moved around. I understand now that this pain was the pain of body parts coming out of dissociation, but I didn't know that then. I wanted Paul to follow and capture that pain and make it go away. I wanted him to squeeze it out of me. But he didn't. I left the session with this vague, annoying pain somewhere between my neck and my thorax along my right shoulder blade. I was annoyed! How could I come into a chiropractor's office with no pain, and leave in pain?

When I got home that night, I continued to reflect on the session, and was moving and breathing into the pain until there was a burst of energy and a flood of tears that I could not staunch. The tears flowed and flowed and I was unable to pinpoint a reason for their appearance. However, as soon the emotional catharsis was complete, and the tears ended on their own accord, the pain was gone. It was completely gone! In its place, I felt a relaxed sense of wellbeing I had not felt in a long time, maybe ever.

"So this is what emotional release feels like," I deduced.

Normally, I invalidated my right to feel whatever I felt. I (and others did as well) judged the intensity of my emotions as unreasonable to the current situation (I would later realize the intensity was traumatic stress, the very distant past seeping into the present). I knew that there was a lot of emotion within me that needed to be released, even if I could not identify the source. I often felt like a ticking bomb lived inside me, ready to explode and destroy me. I frequently felt an urge to rip my skin to soothe an itch deep in my peripheral nerves. But on that night, the flow of tears eased the tension, and I felt calm.

Not sure if I liked the idea of body awareness so much, and wishing my dissociation would return, I still enjoyed the calm after the storm.

I continued for years to use network chiropractic as one of the modalities that helped me heal emotionally. And I can attribute one single network chiropractic event to eliminating my depression and need for psychotropics. Once weaned off, I never felt the need to take another mood-altering medication because whatever had been binding my nervous system into a state of constricted numbness was released.

ꝏ

The Canalis organized an experiential retreat focused on awareness of body rhythms as well as patterns of tension to be released through touch, sound, and energy vibration. It was held in an agricultural area of South Florida at a private home nestled among lush tropical vegetation. A central feature of this oasis was a cold spring pool framed by limestone rocks.

Our day consisted of meditations, including one on vibrational sounds played by Charlene's husband, Qigong practice, an ancient Chinese practice of aligning breath and movement to move energy, or Qi/Chi, through the body, and three network chiropractic sessions spread throughout the day. In between, we soaked in the cool spring to cool off, ate healthy vegetarian foods, and socialized or isolated depending on our individual needs. The idea was to be very aware and honor our own internal rhythms and cues.

I recall a mixture of enjoyment and relaxation blended with anxious pursuit for some great experience that would make me feel better later but not now. I was relaxed but still slightly wired, a coil wound tight and ready to spring. If there are termites in the house, one cannot expect to replace the drywall and paint over it while swarms of insects continue to eat at the foundational core of the structure. The termites must be released or extinguished for the façade to hold. This was me in the 1990s. I could not relax and enjoy the goodness offered by the present moment when a swarm of unprocessed traumatic energy was stuck in my wiring, corroding my nervous system and derailing all other systems (cardiovascular, gastrointestinal, endocrine, immune, musculoskeletal and reproductive).

During the final session of the day, as I lay face down on the table and Paul and Charlene did their tapping and prodding along my spine, an image spontaneously arose in my mind's eye. I did not summon it, nor direct it. It simply appeared out of my subconscious. In the image, my seven-year-old self, a skinny little girl with long brown hair, was fighting off an attacker, pummeling his face with uncontrolled fury and force. As I witnessed the image, my body was flooded with a wave of intense, fiery heat and began trembling, then shaking, then semi-convulsing and sweating profusely. Tears and snot were running down to the floor through the hole in the headrest, and if there were sounds, I recall a keening that pierced the air around me. My saving grace was that I did not try to control this event, even though there was fear, awe, and confusion about what was happening. Instead, I allowed the waves of heat, vibration and sound move through me until I was spent.

I was instructed to not try to think or talk about what happened. I did not need to make sense of it or create a story around it. I did not need to judge the murderous rage that flowed out of me toward another human being who had presumably hurt me in the past. When one is the recipient of an act of aggression, I would come to understand later, our survival instincts kick in and a surge of sympathetic charge, or fight, is mobilized to defend ourselves against the aggressors and insure survival. Until that day, my common response to aggression was to collapse into overwhelming helplessness and suicidal depression. I could not tolerate my instinctive impulse to eviscerate an aggressor I also loved. Now, I had learned that I could express my aggression and channel it for my own protection.

Three women were directed to sit around me while I lay in a bed in a dark, cool room. They laid hands on different parts of my body to contain my grief and provide soothing and comfort. If I tried to speak, they just shushed me.

"Shhh, there's no need to say anything, just rest." Like a newborn, I allowed them to care for me. I let go absolutely and, finally, slept.

We closed the day with an "angel walk" during which we each walked the path between two rows of people with our eyes closed, allowing ourselves to be guided by their hands, to be met at the end by an "angel" who would then situate us on the line. I felt immense gratitude for these supportive, like-minded individuals who were all seeking healing, all wounded healers in their own right. I felt a part of a community, at home, and at peace. That evening I did experience a mild blissfulness, the bliss that emerges after you have wrung all the dirt and grime from a wet towel and hung it out to try.

I cannot recall exactly at what point I stopped using drugs to medicate "depression," but it was soon after that event, because I no longer felt "depressed." My depression, it turns out, was a state of being completely shut down and constricted, with very little energy or breath or life in my body, numb except for the dark dread that cloaks the near dead. All of the energy that had been bound up under the shutdown had moved through and released. It was survival energy that had mobilized but not been utilized when I was overwhelmed as a child. The dark cloak of near-death suffocation has never been felt again since that day. After that day, I began to understand my "depression" as situational, or caused by current events. It never again had the feel of something ancient and insurmountable. Eventually, I discarded all use of psychotropics and have been medication and depression free ever since, the only maintenance required is daily self-care and monitoring to maintain stress levels within my own personal, manageable range.

❧

In conjunction with network chiropractic, I also began working with a Radix psychotherapist. Radix was a popular body-oriented form of psychotherapy in the 1990s. Created by Charles Kelley, PhD, and based on the work of Wilhelm Reich, Radix was an experiential, here-and-now modality that focused on awareness of breath, sensations, body movements, and energy flow. Reich had proposed that one "armors" oneself against the life force in response to overwhelming experiences, and Kelley devised ways to free the life force in order to create a more authentic life. Kelly chose the word "radix" from the Latin word meaning "root" or "source" referring to the force that underlies all movement, feeling and growth.

Joan's office was in a small office building on Sunset Drive. She shared a suite with two others and each office had sound proof double doors. The office was sparse, with a sofa on one end, a lounge chair in the opposite corner, and a mattress in the middle of the floor.

Joan was a small, gentle woman only a few years older than I. Her eyes emanated empathy and kindness, and her presence radiated a sense of peace that I came eagerly every week to find solace from the persisting chaos in my inner and outer life. Even though the sessions were at times excruciatingly painful, I stayed in therapy with Joan for at least five years until she moved to another state.

My strength was my curiosity, which is a critical attribute in mindfulness and a potent antidote to fear. I was a curious observer of my experience and I wanted to understand it, to learn from it. Although the majority of the sessions were experiential, and there was little in the way of talk, at least from Joan, the pieces of the puzzle were coming together.

Radix allowed me to be fully present with what was arising out of my "triggers" without rushing to squelch the energy or emotion with judgments, *shoulds* or *shouldn'ts*, or invalidation, "I'm overreacting and I better button down and get my act together." In Joan's office I allowed myself to fall apart, to express the rage I felt inside, to despair and then repair. Through that process I came to understand that my emotional reactions, especially to the fear of abandonment and rejection that most devastated me, were sourced in very early childhood trauma.

In fact, during one of these sessions, as I felt the exquisite longing that kept me going back to an abusive relationship, I glimpsed the image of an infant no more than eight or nine months old wailing with fury for the mother who refused to come. Standing, her little legs rigid and her back arched to its limit, she gripped the edge of the crib with such force that her pudgy little arms were purple and nearly numb. And yet, mother did not come. These episodes usually ended, I sensed clearly, with me collapsing in exhaustion and visceral hopelessness.

The fact that my mother didn't come when as an infant I needed her was confirmed by the very mother, who told me she didn't want to "spoil me" and therefore left me to cry in my crib, once for so long that I tired of waiting and removed my own diaper. She found me, she recalls, quietly playing with my own stools, which I had smeared all over me and the wall. This same mother also described me as a "terrible baby" who, in her eyes, was responsible for her unhappiness. She had lost forty pounds in the first year of my life, she said, because I needed so much from her that I drained her. The more I needed her, the more she rejected me. The more she rejected me, the more I needed her. We were endlessly locked into a pattern of helplessness and dissatisfaction.

I repeated this pattern in my adult relationships. I needed so much that I was willing to tolerate abuse in my longing to fulfill unmet needs from my early life. This realization didn't immediately make it possible for me to break the pattern, or to maintain a healthy relationship, or even to eliminate the distress caused by separation. But it enabled me to stop blaming and to pursue a different strategy.

I began to have a dialogue with the wailing child inside me with open arms, to soothe her and comfort her and love her despite her need. I stopped hating the part of me that was needy, because my attempts to cut off or disown parts of myself so far had not worked. I began to befriend those ego states that were previously split off. It's an awareness game. If I pushed the experiences away when they arose, they would still rule my behaviors – even if I pretended they weren't there. If I stayed present and observed the experiences, without judgment, the agitation could be metabolized by my body and integrated into my adult self so I no longer needed to regress to a helpless state and act like a child.

During that period, in a meditation group, I spontaneously experienced the image of a light being holding my infant self to its ample bosom. Maybe it was an implicit memory of my great-grandmother, always a comforting figure. The sensation of being held and loved unconditionally was so powerful that I burst into tears of gratitude and relief. I allowed myself to absorb this unconditional love into the very cells of my being, and to accept that I *was* loved. And so the healing evolved gradually, from trusting universal love to gradually beginning to trust the human race.

But it wasn't easy. I would equate the healing process to having surgery without the benefit of anesthesia.

"The bullet hurts more going out than it does going in," a friend once told me. I was undergoing so many changes as I worked through layer upon layer of posttraumatic stress. I was still having nightmares of the abuse from my second husband, recalling and processing childhood abuse memories, and dealing with the stressors of daily life.

With Joan, I worked through memories of abuse, and learned that it was okay to be me, even at my most despairing. I could no longer invalidate or attempt to shut down my emotional and bodily responses. They were valid and had a historical and psychological context. When she left, I returned to a talk therapist to integrate cognitively what I had processed somatically so I could engage in and maintain healthy relationships with the opposite sex and function in life in an emotionally balanced way.

One could say that Joan helped me integrate the developmental links that were missing to the point that I could now talk, and that I entered therapy with Marsha in the adolescent stage of emotional development. I was beginning to see my parents as regular human beings instead of as infallible figures who needed to understand and validate me for me to be okay. Symbolically, I used to have a dream in which my mother was seven feet tall to my five-foot frame (in reality, we are the same height). Mom towered over me and intimidated me, making me feel inadequate and helpless to ever reach up to meet her high expectations.

Marsha was another kind and gentle woman who very skillfully helped me to grow up. I had met her several years earlier when I interviewed for admission to what was then called Project Resolve, a group therapy intervention for survivors of childhood sexual abuse. At that time, she had called the experiences I described as covert sexual abuse, even if I could not specifically recall explicit memories of physical contact -- other than the occasional improper, slobbery kiss by a drunken adult or the tongue in my mouth or dry humping by a rough-housing teenage boy. I had been exposed to sexual images, adult nudity and other unwanted experiences simply because it was the Sixties and my parents were pseudo-hippies who held wild parties were drugs abounded. I attended a group for three months and then had to quit when it became too emotionally overwhelming.

"Of course," she explained. "You cannot process past abuse when you're experiencing abuse in the present." That was the time when I landed in a psychiatric hospital as a result of the verbal and emotional abuse by my eventual second husband. I had developed strong urges to self-harm, so I quit the group because I intuitively knew it was making matters worse.

After we reconnected, Marsha and I worked together for close to a decade. Reviewing our time together as a case study, I can see my progression through the adolescent stages of identity development and the young adult stage of mastering intimacy. She worked from an object relations perspective, which means that we internalize "objects" (or others) based on the subjective experiences we have of them. I needed to internalize a different experience to develop a healthy ego and relate healthily with others in my life. Spiritually, I also needed to have an ego before I could let go of ego.

Marsha was transparent with me, explaining concepts of object relations, such as projective identification, or the act of projecting unwanted aspects of the ego onto others as a defense against anxiety and as a way of communicating internal states to others when words are not possible. She shared articles with me that explained how trauma changes the brain but that therapy also changes the brain. I developed a hopeful view despite my continued struggles to remain regulated in intimate relationships, especially when there was a threat of deep intimacy or a threat of abandonment – both of which equally increased my anxiety.

To summarize a decade of therapy is not an easy task. Suffice it to say that I grew up.

"It's called individuation," she told me once, after I'd related a long story about how I'd finally had an experience where my mother had been critical and it had not affected me. It was a new experience to effortlessly shrug off someone's negative opinion of me because I was clear and content within myself.

"Isn't individuation something that's supposed to happen when you are seventeen?" I was in my early forties by then.

"That's about right," she responded.

"Better late than never!" I quipped. The fact that there was no surge of shame around the idea that I was individuating at such a late stage meant that, indeed, I had individuated.

By then, I could see my mother and her behaviors, or my partner and his behaviors, as reflective of their relational transactions with me – not as a concept that I understood in my head, but as a truth that I experienced in my body. I was not all to blame, nor were they all to blame. We each had played a role. The blaming game was over. As a result, I began to have a sense of humor about myself, and increased compassion for others. In other words, freedom was the ability to stop blaming and to release the stories of the past and their impact on me in the present moment.

Marsha saw me resolve the effects of abuse on my life, make peace with my family, get involved in a healthy relationship with a man I would eventually marry, go through cancer and attend graduate school to become a therapist.

Although I was engaging in the "talking cure," I never stopped seeing body workers as part of my continued healing. Acupuncture, chiropractic, massage, craniosacral, Reiki, meditation, and other modalities became central to my continued wellbeing. They worked so well that I stopped visiting medical professionals altogether. Body, mind and spirit were indeed beginning to join forces to create an optimal environment where dis-ease could not exist. I went from being sickly to being healthy and rarely getting sick. Psychotherapeutic gains were gradually becoming integrated into a new visceral response to life.

❧

I became a believer in acupuncture at sixteen after wisdom tooth surgery. Still in pain and unable to take the prescribed pain killers because I could barely open my jaw to swallow, and if I did they made me nauseous, I enlisted the help of an acupuncturist who rid me of my pain in one single session. More than two decades later, a friend who was completing his acupuncture training offered to give me free treatments to meet his practicum requirements. In essence, I let him use me as a guinea pig in exchange for free services. The treatments were so effective that I moved to very low sliding fee services in his new office when he established a formal practice. He became my primary care physician for a number of years to come and treated me for everything from a viral infection to a broken heart to a fractured pelvis (well, that last one we missed until after he had stuck needles everywhere possible and the pain was still unbearable, so I finally went to an orthopedist to get it diagnosed).

Initially, the treatment focused on emotional symptoms. Sometimes he'd do a treatment to open up my emotions when they were constricted into depression. Other times his treatment would seek to contain the emotions that were spilling everywhere as anxiety or agitation. And it worked. Energetically, something would happen and I would return to work from my lunchtime appointment properly energized or calmed down depending on what was needed that day.

In addition to carefully placed needles, Steve employed every aspect of acupuncture available to him, including moxa, or moxibustion. Moxa consists of burning an herbal (mugwort or *artemesia vulgaris*) mixture directly on the needle or in cone form on acupuncture points along the meridians to move the Qi (or Chi) along the meridians and eliminate stagnation of energy in the blood and the body. I really enjoyed the moxa treatment as anything warming always felt soothing. The only problem with moxa is that you smell as if you've been smoking marijuana. Thankfully no one ever accused me of it when I returned to the office after a treatment.

Another fun acupuncture practice is cupping, whereby Steve placed glass cups along the sides of my spine in such a way that suctioning held the cups in place. Cupping increases blood flow to certain key points, again to increase the flow of Chi along the meridians. The problem with cupping is that sometimes the blood flow would result in perfectly round purple bruises, which led my then-boyfriend to exclaim when he saw my bare back, "Whoa! It looks like the octopus won!"

I give acupuncture credit for restoring balance to my immune system. I went from being constantly sick during the years I was diagnosed as having Chronic Fatigue Syndrome, to not having any illnesses for about five years. When the occasional cold or flu would begin to show symptoms, Steve would place needles along the back of my neck and give me some nasty-tasting Chinese herbs, and the symptoms would quickly peak and subside, allowing me to be more in my life than avoiding life because of a burned out immune system.

Eventually, I added craniosacral therapy, a gentle bodywork method that allows the therapist to access the core of the nervous system, the cerebrospinal fluid, through hands-on manipulation. Developed by osteopathic physician John Upledger in the 1970s, craniosacral therapy was gaining popularity in Miami in the 1990s, when I was introduced to a visiting CST practitioner who was very skilled and went on to become faculty at The Upledger Institute in West Palm Beach.

Cheryl began her sessions by palpating the bones in my skull, gently cradling my cranium in her palms and then moving (purportedly) with the rhythm of the cerebrospinal fluid, which led to supportively moving my body in a way that would unblock impediments to the flow. Every session held, for me, a component of emotional releases, and left me in a deep state of relaxation. But one session in particular left an indelible mark on my consciousness and made me a convinced believer in the mind-body connection, the implicit memory system, and something that would become known today as "interpersonal neurobiology" or mutual self-regulation through attunement.

As Cheryl began to move soothingly from my head, to my neck, and then to my rib cage, I suddenly felt my heart beat and I was transported to an image and a felt sense of being in my mother's womb when, as consciousness first entered my body, I realized I was incarnating. The "voice" inside me yelled loudly and clearly, "Not again!" I felt the unbearable pain and agony of existing as an individualized being separate from the Absolute nondual realm. I came in close contact with the origin of that fierce ambivalence about life that plagued me for as long as I could remember.

These "memories" were implicit, of course, as a fetus does not have the neural capacity yet to consolidate narrative, or explicit memory. They do, however, have the capacity to record implicit memories, and these can be "recalled" as sensorimotor processes through the use of interoception, or the sensitive awareness of one's internal body sensations. Implicit and procedural memories are *nonconsciously encoded,* or recorded in the brain without conscious awareness

"Implicit memory produces habits, physical movements, conditioned emotional responses, and other nonconscious processes," says Dr. Abi Blakeslee in her dissertation on using interoception to access implicit memories, adding that autonomic and emotional states may become conscious via interoception through the awareness of sensations and sensorimotor, or musculoskeletal patterns and behavioral impulses.

Only a few short seconds from that heartbeat, and the piercing pain that followed, Cheryl lifted my right ribcage and shoulder while simultaneously pushing my sacrum forward until I was in a fetal position. Tears streamed down my face as we continued to work in silence, never uttering a single word. Inside, I began to dialogue with that part of me that didn't wish to incarnate, and to make peace with the fact that I had. It was the beginning of a journey that led me on the path of embracing my humanity with joy and appreciation for the gift that it gives us to experience nonduality so pure, undivided consciousness can know itself.

At the end of the session, I asked her, "How did you know I was having a womb experience?"

"I didn't," she replied. "I was only following the spinal fluid and moving you in the position your body wanted to be."

In awe of this powerful healing experience, I continued to explore bodywork and alternative healing modalities, carefully trusting my intuition to rule out quackery and unscrupulous practitioners, of which there are many. Despite the fact that research has not conclusively proven the benefits, or lack thereof, of many emerging healing modalities, those who have benefited and their treatment providers share conclusive anecdotal evidence until a growing body of case studies, and eventually experimental design studies can give us conclusive proof.

Given the fact that the medical and pharmaceutical model is flawed and often has iatrogenic, or unintended negative effects, I feel blessed to have uncovered many effective unconventional approaches to healing my emotional and physical problems. Thanks to weekly psychotherapy, acupuncture, massage and chiropractic sessions, my late thirties to early forties were the healthiest of my life, a life that had been rife with physical and psychological distress.

Reflections

Why embody? For starters, the evidence is mounting that persons with eating disorders – as well as those with past histories of trauma and many with other mental health disorders or psychosomatic diseases--experience disturbances in the experience of their body and sensations leading them to avoid sensory experience by whatever means possible.

In his book *The Divided Mind: the Epidemic of Mindbody Disorders,* John E. Sarno, M.D. attributes a number of psychosomatic illnesses, in particular chronic pain disorders and other autoimmune processes, to this separation of body and psyche. And Stanford biologist Robert Sapolski, in *Why Zebras Don't Get Ulcers,* tells us that the psychologically created stressors that keep our bodies in a chronic stress response are at the root of major illnesses.

Most recently, Dr. Bud Craig has expounded on the importance of interoceptive awareness for optimal self-regulation. In *How Do You Feel? An Interoceptive Moment with your Neurological Self,* he tells us that body awareness is key to mood, emotion and behavior. Our feelings indeed come from the body. They are reported via sensors to the brain's insular cortex for processing and interpretation thereby providing our awareness of emotional, social and all other feelings. In turn, these processes guide our behavior. If we're not aware of what's informing our behavior, we are operating as unconscious beings.

Craig goes on to explain that awareness of interoceptive signals is crucial to understand our decisions and behaviors. He says, "The embodiment theories of emotion emphasize the role of visceral sensation and autonomic activity in the body and brain as a causal source of emotional feelings."

Stephen Porges, whose polyvagal theory of the autonomic nervous system has revolutionized our understanding of these subcortical processes, goes on to say that if we shift physiological states we will be more likely to effect change than if we remain mired in psychological constructs. He coined the term "neuroception" as our nervous system's ability to distinguish safety from threat, positing that most disorders of dysregulation are caused by "faulty neuroception." Because the brain and the body (in particular the heart) are connected via the vagus nerve in a bi-directional regulatory process, by fostering a greater sense of safety at a neurophysiological level, emotional and cognitive perceptions will also shift, allowing us to bond with others and to engage in life productively.

In *Body Sense: The Practice and Science of Embodied Self-Awareness*, Dr. Alan Fogel makes a distinction between conceptual self-awareness and embodied self-awareness, concepts attributed to psychological theorist Donald Winnicott (1896-1971). Winnicott called conceptual awareness the "false" self, and embodied self-awareness the "true" self. He believed embodied awareness, and the capacity to remain present with bodily experience even at its most chaotic, were essential for psychological wellbeing.

Conscious embodiment can help restore the wisdom of the body and support the journey of recovery. The intelligent use of mindfulness (not just any mindfulness, because what you observe is as important as the act of observing when you want to create change) and somatic practices that increase body awareness, assist in the regulation of autonomic hyper-arousal or hypo-arousal, and discharge the 'un-digested' survival energies of trauma, is quickly gaining relevance in the treatment of eating disorders. Yoga, the expressive arts and psychodrama, movement and dance therapies, and integrative mind-body psychotherapies such as Somatic Experiencing® are increasingly available at treatment centers. These approaches increase interoceptive and proprioceptive awareness through the use of sensory-motor tracking skills that strengthen the insula, the anterior cingulate gyrus, and the connections between limbic and cortical areas.

Regardless of the eating disorder presentation, somatic awareness to deepen therapeutic interactions, provide access to disconnected emotions and sensations, and nurture a sense of 'safe' embodiment becomes crucial to healing. Overcoupled and undercoupled aspects of the person's experience -- sensations, images, behaviors, affects, and meanings -- can be gradually integrated to restore a person's sense of wellbeing and resilience. This includes the internal hunger, fullness, and satiety cues necessary to establish long-term recovery and end the dieting, starvation, binge eating, and purging cycles.

Because eating behaviors have been equated with stress at a subcortical, mid-brain level, it makes sense to incorporate practices that take patients 'beyond talk', especially when the reasoning, cortical brain is off-line due to starvation or malnutrition. Since the body is the battleground of the emotions, therapists and their clients might benefit from understanding the language the body is speaking.

The warfare of unmet needs, disowned emotions and disenfranchisement is waged in the body. Body-oriented approaches could be critical in restoring body intelligence and autonomic regulation.

Journaling Exercises

1. What happens when you imagine taking the time to check in with yourself throughout the day to assess your mental, bodily and emotional state?

2. Does it sound scary or helpful?

3. What might you discover when you inquire within and notice thoughts, feelings, sensations and impulses?

4. Can you list ways in which this process of self-awareness could be helpful?

5. Make a list of pleasant sensations you like to experience.

____

____

____

____

____

6. Make a list of unpleasant sensations you don't prefer.

____

____

____

____

____

7. When you become aware of a sensation you do not like, what happens next?

____

____

____

____

____

8. Are there thoughts that increase or decrease the unwanted sensations? List helpful thoughts. List unhelpful thoughts. What happens to the sensations when you place awareness on helpful vs. unhelpful thoughts?

____

____

____

____

____

9. When you notice an uncomfortable sensation, can you find places in your body that are having a more pleasant or neutral sensation? What do you notice when you alternate awareness between the two?

    ____

    ____

    ____

    ____

    ____

10. Think of a time in the last week in which you had a pleasant experience. Recall it in great sensory detail. Now check in with your body and notice what effect the memory is having. Describe the sensations. Now think of a time in the last week in which you had a less pleasant experience. Follow the same procedure. Notice the effect on your body for as long as it feels tolerable, then return to the pleasant memory and see what happens next. Describe your experience.

    ____

    ____

    ____

    ____

    ____

CHAPTER 5

Food for Thought: Food Choices and Their Metaphors

"We, all of us, grave or light, get our thoughts entangled in metaphors, and act fatally on the strength of them." George Eliot, Middlemarch, p. 111

According to Dr. Barbara Birsinger, developer of The Behavior Decoding Method™ designed to uncover the deeper meaning of eating and weight-related behaviors, people's food cravings and body weight behaviors have archetypal and symbolic meanings that need to be decoded in order to excavate their intended purpose and positive outcome.

Personally, I was drawn to sweet and milky substances, particularly rich, creamy and full-fat ice creams with no artificial flavors or colorings, or velvety cream-rich cheese cakes. It's as if my body and my soul needed to be nourished, deeply, into the cells of my being. On the one hand, I was firing through life in a frantic attempt to achieve perfection through intellectual overstimulation and by molding my body into a biologically-impossible shape. On the other hand I was exhausted, chronically dissatisfied and endlessly drained of life physically, mentally and emotionally.

I needed to feed my body with what my cells really craved, and my emotional self with the unconditional sweetness of food. My mind required the empty numbing accomplished as I shifted my awareness simply to the act of letting the food textures swirl around in my mouth and absorbing the tastes through the buds in my tongue until they exploded in a celebration of pleasure in the deep folds of my brain. Until, that is, the associated panic would set in and I would be flooded with images of fat cells reproducing underneath my skin and making me fat, which would rapidly cascade into an uncontrollable urge to expel the culprit from my viscera, leaving me once again depleted but at peace. I was then ready to repeat the pattern – restrict, deplete, desire, fulfill, reward, stuff, panic, purging and numbness.

Dr. Stephen Porges' polyvagal theory of emotions, attachment, communication and self-regulation proposes a three-tiered autonomic nervous system based on evolutionary survival requirements. These neurobehavioral systems for prosocial and defensive survival responses are mediated by the vagus nerve, which also acts as a primary regulator of the gut. The most "modern" version of this vagal regulatory mechanism is mediated by the nerves and muscles of the face, neck and ears, and is first activated in infants through the feeding process. As the infant matures, this system evolves to promote social engagement behaviors by engaging the "vagal break" that dampens the sympathetic defensive mobilization, thereby calming the heart. It makes sense, then, that engaging chewing and swallowing actions would soothe our activation.

I am now convinced that my food choices had a lot to do with my insecure attachment patterns. In her book, *The Impact of Attachment*, Danish psychologist Susan Hart categorizes eating disorders in relation to three hierarchical structures of the brain and autonomic nervous system. Dr. Hart theorizes that eating disorders are related to severe dysregulation. She states that when infants are unable to achieve balance in the autonomic functions of the nervous system, and the parent did not provide sufficient regulation through their interactions with the child, the child has trouble managing the feeding and digestive processes, which rely on autonomic functions.

Because self-regulation structures in the right brain only form after birth through a securely attached, attuned interaction between child and caregiver, those who had ruptures in attachment have immature limbic and cortical structures. One in particular, the insula, is responsible for decoding sensory information. Damage to the insula in the right hemisphere destroys awareness of bodily states. This creates an inner sense of "emptiness" that is nothing more than the interrupted sensory pathways.

In fact, research now confirms that obesity is not just influenced by metabolic rate and excess calories, but it's also affected by the neural regulation of hunger and satiety. Therefore understanding how the nervous system regulates feeding behaviors is key, and the central gustatory system is at the heart of these neural structures. A distributed brain circuit that integrates peripheral sensory information from multiple sensory channels with endocrine and gastrointestinal signals, the central gustatory system participates in the detection and discrimination of tastes and smells, allowing for the selection of nutrients and rejection of toxic compounds. Additionally, these somatosensory systems discriminate odor, texture, and temperature, which participate, with taste, in the perception of flavor.

Taste processing also has emotional and reward components that constitute part of a highly complex circuitry that integrates multisensory gustatory input with homeostatic and reward signaling, general arousal, directed motivation, and neuronal mechanisms for motor, autonomic, and endocrine responses.

Another hit to the ability to sense information to and from the gut happens with stimulation of the vagus nerve, which influences feelings of fullness and satiety after a meal. This vagal response seems to become desensitized when binge eating on large quantities of food is frequent, reducing the binge eater's capacity to recognize fullness. Bulimics, on the other hand, will miss the fullness cue and then feel an autonomic urge to expel the food because this emetic response has become conditioned. This explains the difficulties persons with bulimia have in maintaining recovery.

Scientists also hypothesize that sugar stimulates the release of opioids, which in turn soothes both physical and emotional pain. Eating can soothe loneliness because it activates neural pathways related to social contact, Hart reports. She quotes scientific research that have demonstrated that feeding sugar water to mice prematurely separated from their mothers reduces their separation distress calls.

Personally, I seemed to have been stuck in this infantile state, having trouble detecting basic sensory input, including hunger and satiety, stuffing myself to the point of vomiting, and seeking hungrily for the sweet milk that would soothe my distress. Whether biochemically or symbolically, sweetened milk provided a comfort that I paradoxically sought out but also rejected. Hart has an explanation for this as well. She states that anorexia and bulimia develop in part to attempt autonomic control of disorganized or anxious states, and in part as "massive introverted aggression."

Bodily, aggression is expressed by chewing and biting in infants and toddlers. We clench out jaws when we are angry, and chewing on what one of my clients called "crunchy and convenient" food products provides some autonomic discharge of the stifled sympathetic charge of aggression. If I can't tell you that I am angry, or I cannot allow myself to be angry, I just may chew my way through an entire bag of crunchy chips.

Food also may evoke pleasant memories at an implicit, or subconscious level. I remember a time when I binged on mixed nuts. Upon later reflection, I recalled first eating that fancy mix at the home of my German grandparents in Nicaragua, which provided an escape from the mundane and stressful experiences at my house. When we visited them it was like going on a fancy vacation and eating new and exciting foods. The fat content in the nuts, the chewing motion in my jaw, and the pleasant memories elicited by the taste and texture of the food all contributed to a more positive affective state.

And let's look at taste and smell, which are closely related in our physiological "gustatory" processing and have strong emotional associations. Sweet, sour, bitter, and salty each may be used to express equivalent feelings. This is why we speak of "dis-gust" when we don't like something or find it "unpalatable." We say "you are so sweet," when someone does something nice for us. On the other hand, we speak of bitterness when someone has angered us. We might also indicate that someone finds something distasteful by noting that they had a "sour expression."

We might refer to people as "a rotten egg" to indicate their badness, or as "cool as a cucumber" when their disposition is unemotional. Or we'll qualify movement with expressions such as "slow as molasses." We associate plainness with "vanilla" and someone exotic as "spicy." Similarly, we associate goodness with pleasant scents, as in "the sweet smell of success," or badness with unpleasant smells, as in "your idea stinks."

We also use metaphors that implicate ingestion, digestion or expulsion, as in:

That's food for thought. Let me chew on it for a while.
That was difficult to swallow.
Don't shove your beliefs down my throat.
I'm just digesting what was said.
The students regurgitated what they've memorized.
I'm stewing
It's eating at me
He's spoon-feeding them the information.
That's a pretty shitty thing to do.
He's pissing away the family fortune.
My stomach sank when I heard that
It felt like a punch in my gut
I carry the weight of the world on my shoulders

Finally, let's look at specific foods and food groups and their hypothesized influence on various neuro-physiological systems.

Sweets and starches seem to be commonly sought-after foods for bingeing. Baked goods and cereals, French fries and pasta feature on many a binge eater's repertoire. Nutrition specialists point to a serotonin release function. When serotonin increases, mood improves. We get feelings of wellbeing and inner calm.

Meats and dairy, on the other hand, increase dopamine and reduce cortisol. Dopamine makes us more alert and able to concentrate. Cortisol is a hormone released by the adrenals under stress, which when overactive reduces serotonin. Dietary fats in turn produce endorphins which reduce our awareness of pain and increases a sense of pleasure.

Independent of subjective feelings we might have associated with particular food tastes and nutritional content, new studies show that hormones in our digestive system appear to communicate directly with our brains. In an environment where people were fed directly through a tube, saturated fat appeared to reduce negative emotions. Research subjects reacted with less sadness to listening to sad music and viewing sad faces if their bellies were full of saturated fat versus a simple saline solution. This speaks to the biological beyond the psychological. It also contradicts the idea that we should eat a low-fat diet. Instead, by eating healthy fats we could be improving our moods and needing to binge less on "false" fast foods that don't provide satiety.

Journaling Exercises

1. Think of the particular foods that you most crave. Bring to your awareness all of the qualities of that food as you see it, smell it and taste it. What do you want? What would having that do for you?

   ____

   ____

   ____

   ____

   ____

2. When you identify the functions of eating that particular food, what does it give to you that you can't get in any other way? What does it take away that is valuable to you?

____

____

____

____

____

3. What would happen if you could get what that food choice gives you in other, non-eating disorder ways? Would you try it? Why or why not?

____

____

____

____

____

4. What might you lose if you attain what you desire without relying on your eating disorder behavior or food choice?

____

____

____

____

____

5. Describe some of the needs that your food choices are fulfilling, e.g. the nightly pint of ice cream you eat for comfort after visiting a dying relative in the hospital.

____

____

____

____

____

6. Describe some of the problems that choosing food to fulfill non-nutritional needs is creating for you?

____

____

____

____

____

7. When you balance what you are receiving vs. what you are losing or the problems you are creating by using food for emotional needs, which end of the balance wins out?

____

____

____

____

____

8. What are the pros and the cons of continuing the problematic eating behavior?

____

____

____

____

____

9. What are the pros and the cons of eliminating the problematic eating behavior?

____

____

____

____

____

10. What are your favorite food metaphors?

CHAPTER 6

Finding the Middle Path: The Dialectics of Food, Eating & Exercise

ALTHOUGH PARTIALLY RECOVERED IN TERMS of eating habits, I still experienced a great level of body image distress well into my thirties and worked hard to maintain a low body weight and pound my shape into something I found semi-acceptable. As my health improved, I began to exercise more and to engage in more intense athletic endeavors. When it came to exercise, I did not know the middle path.

Throughout elementary, middle school and high school, I shunned exercise, preferring to sit on the sidelines reading a book. In my twenties and thirties, I was a "gym rat," spending hours daily at the gym. At thirty-nine, I started to run after a friend told me she had lost ten pounds without altering her food intake while training to run a half-marathon.

"Aha!" I thought, "There's the exercise for me."

I joined an organized running group through a local athletic shoe store called Footworks.

The first time I ran three miles with their weekday evening group, I thought I was going to die. My thighs became itchy and red within a few short miles, my muscles quite unused to receiving such an intense flow of blood and oxygen. My lungs burned and my breath was raspy, but one the group members told me he was sixty and had just run his first marathon. I was not even forty, so I could not quit. I was encouraged to continue and I felt quite happy to have completed the run.

I continued to do training runs with a group of women who gathered every morning at five-thirty at "the circle" near the entrance to Coconut Grove. It was a motley crew that included a Welsh and a South African. At first I had trouble keeping up, but soon I began to run faster than all of them – not that I ever ran very fast at all, but I improved from a slow twelve-minute mile to a racing speed that was closer to eight minutes in a short race and ten minutes in a marathon. Daily, I woke up at five with just enough time to brush my teeth, chug a cup of coffee and get my running gear on. We would run five to six miles and in an hour be back in our cars heading home to shower, change and head to work.

Running fever was epidemic in Miami. Articles about couch potatoes turning into marathon runners abounded. It was hard not to catch the bug, with the thrill of endorphins flooding me every run I did. Not to mention the added incentive that I had started dating a fabulous and dedicated runner who could run a 5K (3.1 miles) in seventeen minutes plus a few seconds. So I enrolled to run my first marathon, and I would make it a good one. Paris! Why not? I would run *Le Maraton de Paris* in the spring of 2002 at the age of forty. I began training in earnest.

"You can't run a marathon without the help of a nutritionist," my running friends told me, demanding that I visit a registered dietitian if I wanted to be successful and maintain my recovery. I thought it would be a good idea, since I was abstaining from any processed sugars and I was hesitant to use the carbohydrate gels everyone was touting. So I made an appointment with Lisa, who treated eating disorders and was known as "the runners' nutritionist."

"You're an athlete now," Lisa told me, which elicited quite a chuckle from me because, despite the miles, I did not consider myself athletic. "You cannot do this race without using gels." She prescribed one gel at forty-five minutes and one gel every thirty minutes after that.

To the detriment of all the residents we probably woke up with our loud and boisterous chatter, I ran three times a week before dawn with the group. You forget the world is asleep when you're getting a runner's high. Then I added long runs on Saturdays with an organized group that matched my pace, about eleven minute miles at the time. The length of those Saturday runs increased gradually until a ten mile run was the minimum and eighteen or twenty-two miles was common as we neared the marathon's date: April 7, 2002.

In the meantime, I began to run every single half-marathon available in South Florida. In Naples that winter, I ran my best time to date: 1:56:00, which put me at 34th in my age group and 564th overall out of about 1300 runners; not impressive but respectable for a new and older runner like me. It had been a beautiful race meandering through shaded, tree-lined residential streets where residents hosed us down with their sprinklers and offered slices of oranges with their encouraging cheers.

I had pushed myself, and although proud of my accomplishment, the next day I paid the price. On a gentle three mile run I noticed my groin hurt. It was an annoying pain that seared into my pubis with every pouncing step, but I assumed it was residual soreness from the previous day's race that would eventually go away. So I continued to train, week after week, forty miles per week on average, taking Advil and stretching my hip flexors and adductors in complete denial of the injury. One day, after a twenty mile run that I completed by swallowing little brown pill after little brown pill and stretching at every water break, I found myself unable to walk because every step sent such a sharp stab of pain into my hip that I couldn't step on my left foot anymore.

I stopped running for a few days, and I was having acupuncture needles stuck in every possible part of my body except my perineum, which I would forever refuse to do. Still, I was crawling up to the second floor in my two-story townhouse, pulling myself up with my arms, because I could not walk up a set of stairs. I started using a pair of crutches that I had in storage, and stopped running for a few days to see if the pain would subside.

My corporate job required me to travel to the Far East in preparation for the 2002 World Cup, which the company was sponsoring. In Tokyo one month before the marathon, a walk to the Imperial

Gardens made me realize the error of my ways. I cried in pain as I made my way back to the Imperial Hotel on a Sunday afternoon. I called home to urgently make an appointment with an orthopedic specialist for the day after I returned. A simple X-ray confirmed a double fracture in the *pubic ramus*. He showed me where the bones had started to fuse. Further imaging using magnetic resonance, or MRI, revealed that the adductors (the muscles in the inner thighs) were torn and had probably pulled on the pubis thus stretching the area until it broke.

"How in the world did you do that?" he asked, "that's not a very common runner's injury."

"Nothing I ever do is common," I answered.

I walked on crutches for the next six months. Indeed, I walked on crutches to *Le Maraton de Paris* and watched the winner finish with a time of 2:08:00 and throw his smelly sneakers to the audience as part of his celebratory dance. I saw my team members, all of whom had been training to raise funds for The Wellness Community of Greater Miami (a free cancer resource and support center), run and finish the marathon with various completion times. I walked on crutches in the Champs Elysées, to the Arc de Triomph, the Musée d'Orsay, the Eiffel Tower, and the Jardins de Versailles. But I did not run a marathon. At least not until June 2003, when I finally made it to Grandma's Marathon in Duluth, Minnesota, where I ran with seven thousand other runners for twenty-two miles along the stunning beauty of Lake Superior to enter town and complete the 26.2 miles with a chip time of 4:13:06.

Between 2003 and 2005 I ran five marathons and more than twenty half-marathons, among many other 5K and 10K races. I was probably running about one race per week. My personal record was 4:09:01 in the 2004 Miami Marathon. My 5K times went from 30:38 in February 2001 to under twenty-five minutes in 2005. And because you can't outrun your soul, cancer stopped me in my tracks.

Reflections

I went from being a gangly, uncoordinated youth who dreaded recess and physical education through elementary school and high school, to exercising up to twelve hours a week in my thirties and forties, to barely being able to walk for more than ten minutes on days when chemo fatigue got the best of me. I was a master of the extremes. *Always* feeling tired and *never* wanting to exercise to the reverse. I saw the world in black and white, and nowhere was this pattern more evident than in my eating. During the worst periods of my eating disorder, I was either starving or binge eating. Even small meals where to be avoided, and when I ate, I ate until it hurt.

When we live in the extremes, we are prone to cognitive distortions. The words *always* and *never* permeate our vocabulary. We catastrophize even the smallest incidents. A bounced check augurs bankruptcy. Neck pain must signal meningitis and a headache a brain tumor. An innocent slight by another person means they hate us. Even having a partner turn away from us in bed to get comfortable is interpreted as a major rejection.

No therapy is better suited to treat these symptoms of cognitive, emotional, behavioral and interpersonal dysregulation as Dialectical Behavior Therapy, designed by Dr. Marsha Linehan, who herself suffered immensely as a young woman from these extremes of thinking, feeling and behaving.

While DBT was developed specifically for work with borderline personality disorder, a disorder of extreme dysregulation possibly sourced in early attachment trauma that causes an individual to become easily activated in the presence of another human being, it has been studied and proven effective as a treatment intervention for bulimia and binge eating, which also are disorders of dysregulation. DBT is less effective with anorexia, which is considered more of a disorder of over-control, but a modified DBT program called Radically Open DBT (RO-DBT) seems to be better suited to address the symptoms of over-control exhibited in anorexia.

Bulimia and binge eating have been described as maladaptive emotion regulation strategies, wherein binge eating and purging is used to temporarily relieve an aversive emotional state with its associated thoughts and sensations. It appears that improving skills in emotional regulation improves outcomes for individuals with bulimia and binge eating disorder.

A 2014 study of a guided self-help DBT program for individuals with binge eating disorder demonstrated at six-month follow up that reported improvements in emotion regulation were associated with binge abstinence.

Emotion regulation is characterized by the ability to tolerate extreme affect and to regulate one's affect. In one study of women with co-occurring borderline personality and bulimia or anorexia who had failed to respond to previous treatment, self-rated eating-related complaints and general psychopathology, as well as ratings on global psychosocial functioning, were significantly improved at post-treatment and at follow-up.

These and other studies provide support for the theoretical role of binge eating as an emotion regulation strategy, and conversely, why improved self-regulation reduces eating disorder symptoms.

So what does dialectical mean? The dictionary states that dialectics is the art or practice of arriving at the truth by the exchange of logical arguments, which means that every opposing view holds a kernel of truth and it is in the synthesis of thesis and antithesis that one finds truth. Conflict is resolved by seeing the truth in each of the opposing ideas.

Dialectics also posits that no object could hold together without an opposing object to hold it in place. It's like the saying, "It takes two to tango." There is no atom if the electrons fly away. The whole needs all of its parts to be a whole. We need to feel hungry in order to eat and survive. When we experience grief, we also can experience the fullness of joy. A life of wholeness includes both.

Dialectics views change as gradual. It is in the dance between these two opposing forces that the scales tip one way or another. To influence change in one direction, one must move toward the middle, rather than fluctuate between the extremes. Dialectics also argues that change is cyclical, but that these cycles do not come back exactly to where they started; they don't make a perfect circle. Instead, change is evolutionary, moving in a spiral. Even tiny changes, over time, tip the scale in one direction or another.

The dialectics of eating disorders are outlined in the graph below, which was developed by the patients of a DBT eating disorder skills training group I ran in Miami, Florida. It is common for a person with an eating disorder, for example, to feel hopeless after making progress and experiencing a lapse in symptoms, such as a binge or binge-purge episode. "I am back at square one!" they'll cry out, and proceed to decompensate. When viewed dialectically, one can view lapses as part of the evolutionary spiral of recovery, events to learn and grow from rather than a return to illness. Unfortunately spirals can go down as well as up. Of course, we want recovery to be an upward spiral.

Another common dialectical impasse in binge eating disorder, for example, is "I want to eat chocolate cake (replace with your favorite guilty food pleasure)" but "I want to avoid chocolate cake because I want to lose weight." Many binge eating or overweight clients feel bound by rigid dieting rules while also feeling unable to make a commitment to let go of binge foods. These rigid dieting rules, on one extreme of the dialectic, set them up for relapse because they are eating in a way that is not sustainable. On the other end of the dialectic, once the diet has taxed their bodies or their resolve, they swing into eating chocolate cake as if it is the last time chocolate cake will be available on earth. The dialectical solution would be, "I can eat chocolate cake on occasion and in moderation, even when I am trying to lose weight."

The main dialectic in DBT is the dialectic of acceptance vs. change. When we are focusing only on change, there is dissatisfaction with things as they are, causing suffering. If we focus only on acceptance, there may not be enough emphasis on change, and change is often necessary if we are to suffer less. Dialectics provides the tool that gives you the wisdom to work steadily and patiently for change--building the side you want to win, studying how much farther you need to go and what you need to do to make a turning point.

As Japanese Zen Master Shunryu Suzuki-roshi said:

"All of you are perfect just as you are and you could use a little improvement."

Dialectical Conflicts in Eating Disorders

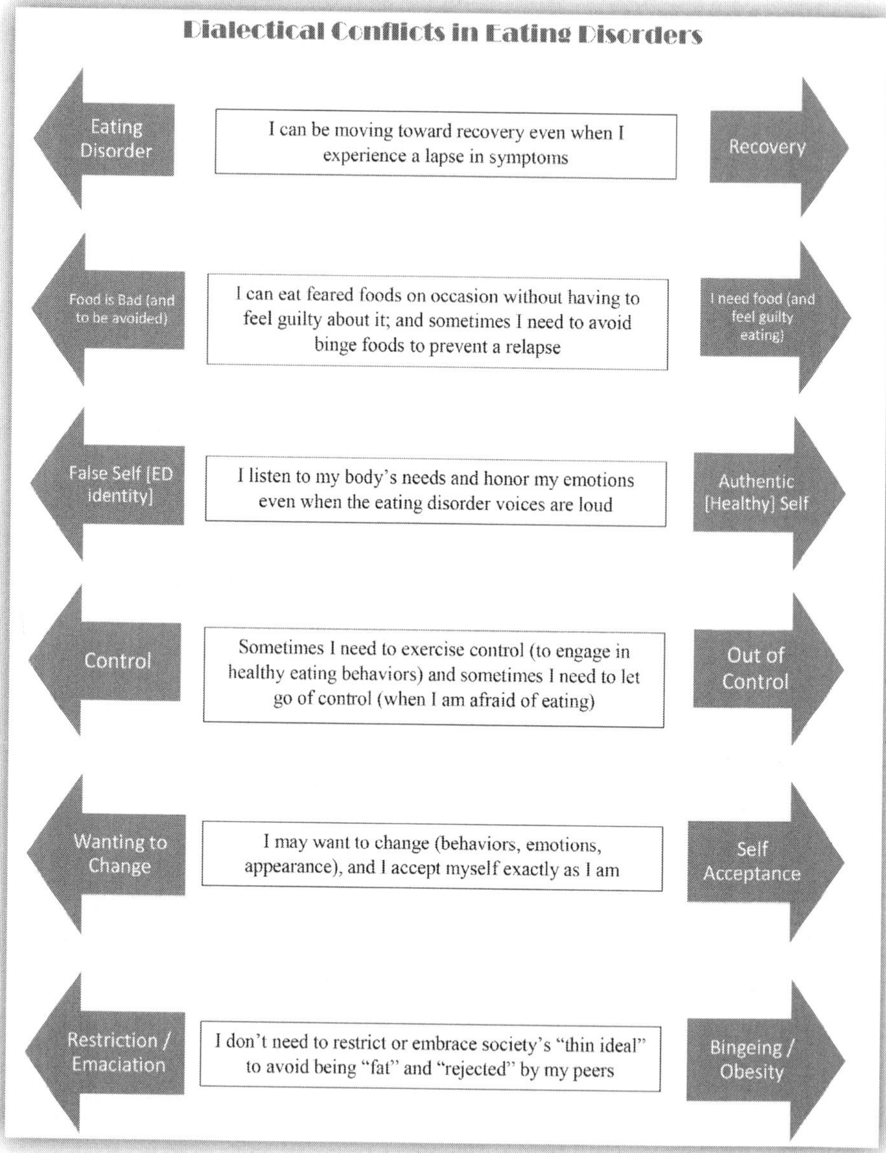

Journaling Exercises

1. Identify one of your eating disorder behaviors, e.g. skipping a meal, overeating, purging, and exercising excessively. Think of the last time you used that behavior. Identify the thoughts, feelings (desired and actual) and unmet needs at the time of the behavior.

____

____

____

____

____

2. Repeat the process for each of the eating disorder behaviors you practice.

____

____

____

____

____

3. What is the intended positive outcome of the behavior, e.g. self-soothing, venting discomfort, eliciting sleep, etc.?

____

____

____

____

____

4. What are non-eating disordered ways you already know or use to achieve the same outcomes?

____

____

____

____

____

5. How can you transform the intended effect of the eating disorder behavior into self-care strategies, effective communication strategies or crisis survival skills that provide a similar effect without the unintended consequences?

____

____

____

____

____

6. Once you have identified the dialectical extremes that your eating disorder symptoms occupy, can you practice radical self-acceptance? If not, why not?

____

____

____

____

____

7. How can you begin to take small, gradual steps in the direction of the change you want to see? Can you be content with patient improvement? If not, why not?

____

____

____

____

____

8. Write the pros and cons of acceptance.

____

____

____

____

____

9. Write the pros and cons of change.

____

____

____

____

____

10. Where do the above pros and cons intersect? Is there an opportunity to move in the direction of a middle path? What is the middle path for your particular situation?

____

____

____

____

____

CHAPTER 7

Breathing in Life, A Spoonful at a Time: The Role of Breath

❧

AT THE DARKEST HOUR, WHEN I should have been sleeping, I am reliving the conversation I had with my boyfriend earlier that evening on the hallway payphone in the psychiatric unit at Larkin Hospital in South Miami. *You're a psycho, and I'm not going to put up with your bullshit anymore.* I can't get a word in as he hurls these insults at me. I am mute with disbelief, or frozen with hopelessness that I will ever be loved in the way that I long for, unconditionally, wholly and completely.

The more I listen, the more despondent I become, a visceral gnawing chewing through my intestinal cavity until I am gutted and empty. *How did I get here?* I think. Logically, I know that I wouldn't be "psycho" if it wasn't for the fact that he has been on a two-week manic stretch that left me so weary and bone tired that I ended up sitting on our bathroom floor contemplating all the psychiatric drugs I could take to kill myself. His, mine, ours. I am thirty, and I want to die.

His pills were among the ones I was contemplating taking. Pills it seems, is the main, if not only, tool in the medical arsenal against problems of human distress. Thus far, they have not tamed my depression, an intense melancholy first noticed at age twelve and sourced in the well of a deep self-pity that is fed by the river of *my mother doesn't love me.*

So here I am, in the psych ward. And there he is, still on the loose, torturing me through the phone line because I can't bear to be disconnected from him. All I want is to feel secure in someone's love. How we went from talking about shopping for an engagement ring, to him waking me up at five in the morning on Valentine's Day to tell me he couldn't marry me because I was a *worthless piece of shit* is beyond my capacity to comprehend right now. Why I still want him baffles me even more.

John, be reasonable, I plead with him, trying to convince him that, in his right mind, he would remember how much he loves me. I *need* him to remember. I long for him to be more like the husband who comes to visit his catatonic wife every evening, and sits patiently whispering loving words in her ear and spooning pudding in her mouth even as she sits there, unresponsive and mute. I watch her coming back to life, day by day, as she recognizes the voice of her lover and rejoins the living to be with him. She blooms right in front of my curious eyes, less from the electroconvulsive shock treatment than from the watering of his nurturing murmurs.

This is my fantasy, the musings of a thirty-year-old woman who has pursued that love from a mother who was as elusive as empty ghosts. Except I didn't give up. *It's never too late to want your mother,* my first therapist had once said to me. I had only transferred my vain attempts to acquire love, in the way I wanted it, from my mother to the string of men who populated my life from the age of thirteen. I fell in love only with those whose love was unavailable or unattainable, as if to remind me of the unworthiness in which I had come to clothe myself, daily, deliberately.

My mother has not visited me in this hospital. She refuses to participate in any therapy since my last hospitalization three years earlier at a residential treatment center for eating disorders, where she stormed out after the family therapist inquired about her role in the development of my bulimic symptoms.

I will not be blamed! Her fury leaving an upturned chair and a tail of cold disdain.

It's just as well that she's not involved, I tell myself. But secretly I still hope she will want to understand me, hold me tight, and comfort my distress. Validation is not a skill she possesses, however. At this hospital where I am now, she sends a card. On the front, it reads: *Stupid, Selfish, Insensitive, Inconsiderate, Thoughtless and Ungrateful.* Inside: *But Forgiven.*

I want to believe that she means well. I want to believe that I am forgiven, although I am not sure for what transgressions. A part of me knows this is not the card you send to someone contemplating suicide. Another part wonders what she was thinking. Now that my marijuana-growing, post-smoking, hippie-wanna-be artist mother has turned into a rabid born-again Christian, her grasp of reality seems to be even more elusive. She'll whack you over the head with the bible but exercise few of the principles taught by the man-God she claims to worship.

I am going to cut you up into sixty-four little pieces!

Only days before my hospitalization, she had yelled these words at me after she found out I had taken my son, her only grandchild, to therapy. My mother does not believe in therapy.

It is brainwashing, she says.

I am aware that my brain, as it is, needs a good washing, twisted and distorted by trauma until I cannot perceive the good that life has to offer, aware only of the threat of abandonment or harm. And tonight, the words that keep spinning through my head in this wash cycle are, *my husband hates me and my mother wants me dead.* With each spin-cycle, my agitation increases. It is as if a trillion needles are piercing every millimeter of skin and an invisible fist is crunching my trachea. Soon the words in my head transform into *I have to do something, I have to do something, and I have to do something.*

That something is rip the skin off my body to stop the prickling because I cannot, in any imaginable universe, scream or wail or vomit violently enough to empty the molten lava that is burning inside me.

Despite the watchful eye of nurses and mental health technicians milling about the island where they have their work stations, I find a way to cut myself. I am heaving and hyperventilating, my fists clenching and unclenching with a certainty that I have to fiercely scratch something and a feverish confusion that freezes me. I desperately look around the room. There is nothing. They took all scissors, razors, and even my shoelaces when I came in a few days before on a Sunday night, but I find a plastic make-up case that holds my blush. It takes a few tries, but I manage to crack the transparent plastic cover in half and begin to scratch my forearms with the sharp edges. It's not sharp enough to create an open wound, but I manage to scratch hard enough that the redness is giving way to some droplets of blood. It burns, and the physical pain begins to soothe the despair that was gutting me.

A nurse finds me on my bed and stops me. She yanks me up from my bed and takes me to the nursing station, where they call my psychiatrist, Dr. Vilasuso. He prescribes a shot of liquid Thioridazine, brand-name Mellaril, a common antipsychotic used to suppress agitation. Almost immediately, I am bathed in a calm warmth that causes me to become pleasantly drowsy. It's a whole-body sensation that I like and makes me think that maybe I could create scenes like this again just so I can receive this drug. I recognize this thought as coming from an addict's mind and a voice of sanity intervenes. *No,* it says, *you will not do this again just to get drugs.* I self-harmed again, but this was the one and only time I required an anti-psychotic to tranquilize me.

In the morning, I am weighed – ninety-four pounds – and my vitals are taken – ninety-seven over fifty-eight. My temperature is not much over ninety-seven degrees. My pulse? Who knows? It could be high, or it could be low, but it does not have much variability.

Recovery from my eating disorder has taken the shape of a restrictive meal and exercise plan that I cannot deviate from without needing to purge, much like when I was in kindergarten and coloring outside the lines sent me into a sweaty panic. The tyranny of perfectionism has ruled me with a firm grip and my parameters are very slim. They are meant to wind me tight so I can contain the despair that lives in me. I am even unable to follow the guided progressive muscle relaxation exercises because as soon as I begin to relax, even one percent, I crumble into fragments, cry, and shake. Because no one says *it's okay to cry and shake,* I lie on my bed fantasizing that I slice my arms with razor blades -- to release, through the rivulets of fiery red blood, the steam of rage and fury and terror that inhabit my body.

They give me a plastic gallon jug that I am supposed to pee in for the next twenty-four hours. *We're testing your cortisol levels*, they tell me. For the rest of the day, I mingle about with the other patients, a disparate gang of crazies who spend their time playing board games in the main room, smoking on the concrete roof-top patio, or gluing glitter on Keds shoes during *art therapy*.

Danny, bipolar and coming off a manic episode, saunters up to me in the hallway tapping his fingers incessantly and whispering to himself. He is as loud as his fiery red hair and big freckles, the nervous energy visible in his tense, skinny frame. He tells me he only slept two hours the night before. Eventually he will crash, and then hopefully stabilize and be released. He walks over to the "med" dispensing station and tips a little plastic cup over, emptying the contents on his tongue like morning communion. He turns and bumps into María, a Puerto Rican self-declared psychic.

"Watch it, they're trying to poison us," Danny says to her.

"Danny! Come back here!" The nurse yells out. She asks him to open his mouth, and checks under the tongue. There they are, two little pills, both pink, one a tablet and one a capsule. "Danny, you know better than that," she scolds, in an irritated voice. "This is medicine, not poison. We're trying to help you feel better."

He swallows the pills. He glares at her and scurries away, still tap-tapping his fingers in a Morse code comprehensible only to him. María stirs up trouble daily, claiming to be a *Santería* witch who can foretell the future (and who can say she can't). She had become violent during a psychotic episode and was court-mandated into the unit until she is stable enough to not be a threat to herself or society. María is always watching the other patients interact with their visitors and sharing her "visions" with them.

María has become obsessed with the relationship difficulties that landed me in the psych ward. She seeks me out after my visits and tells me, "You like him because he's exciting; your ex-husband bored you." She's cunningly correct. Exciting, indeed. An unstable, unfaithful, violent man diametrically different from my introverted, schizoid first husband.

I am locked up with this strange cast until the staff is assured that I will move out from John's apartment and away from danger. My best friend Clara, notifies our support group: *Inge wanted to kill herself, but at least she didn't drink.* I don't drink, and I don't kill myself, but I am a long way from sane judgment and emotional balance, my only guide a still small inner voice of sanity that keeps me moving toward the light, questioning the prescriptions of the mental health system and holding out for a healing that is complete and unlimited. I limp along, crippled by hunger and the ambivalence that causes me to still contemplate dying as a way out from having to live a life that feels too painful.

Rubén Darío, the iconic Nicaraguan poet who revolutionized Latin American literature and died an alcoholic, sang the praises in his poetry of "a tree, barely sensitive, and the stone, hard because it no longer feels; because there is no greater pain than being alive, nor bigger sorrow than the sentient life." In these poetic stanzas he captured the essence of my discontent at being born into this conscious life in a country about to be torn by war, a nation mythically known as the land of poets, drunks and rebels.

As far back as I can remember, my ambivalence about being alive was there. I was like a burn victim with raw skin, just too sensitive. Everything hurt. Nothing soothed. I felt afraid and alone. As I ponder the source of this hypersensitivity to negative emotions, my imagination takes me to my mother's womb. I imagine the crushing darkness around my developing fetus, capillaries irrigating my tissues. I imagine that I knew, even then, that I did not want to be confined to this world. Being embodied felt like a prison to be endured rather than enjoyed, a separation from everything good, and an alienation from the spirit realm.

These conflicting impulses – to be here or to depart from this life, to bond or not to bond, to belong or reject belonging -- emerged in infancy and seemed to tug at me throughout my life. I walked a tightrope between the longing to be embodied and the yearning to become disembodied, filled with shame at the hint of pleasure. Dissociation, disconnection, and disembodiment were common experiences, even experiences I sought out through drugs, alcohol, food, and by seeking transcendental experiences. Anything to avoid feeling the tautness in my skin and the raw nerve endings that populated it.

To avoid feeling, I became a master in constricting my breath. Breathing as little as possible tightened the grip against the flood of feelings and sensations that breathing in too deeply provoked. Breathing exercises sent me reeling into chaos and uncontrollable weeping.

Reflections

Breathing exercises, such as diaphragmatic belly breathing, can be very helpful to some. To others, it could be a recipe for disaster to invite too much breath in at once.

The more current understanding of the autonomic nervous system is that it is a system organized hierarchically for survival. Dr. Stephen Porges, a neuroscientist now on faculty at the University of North Carolina at Chapel Hill, developed a theory of the autonomic nervous system as a set of hierarchically organized neural circuits involved in the regulation of autonomic states for the purpose of survival. The theory led to the discovery of three phylogenetically ordered neural circuits and an interpretation of autonomic reactivity as adaptive. According to Porges, the parasympathetic nervous system, which is mediated by the Xth cranial nerve known as the vagus nerve, has two branches: a newer mammalian circuit linking the heart to the face for social engagement functions, and a more ancient, potentially lethal branch responsible for the defensive responses of immobility.

The polyvagal theory provides a plausible explanation for hard-wired responses during stress and observed in several psychiatric disorders, including eating disorders. The theory holds that there is a hierarchy of responses, where the most primitive systems (dorsal vagal immobility) are activated only when the higher-order structures of sympathetic activation or ventral vagal social engagement fail. These neural pathways that regulate autonomic states are also responsible for the expression of emotional and social behavior. Therefore, the physiological state is a substructure of emotion and behavior and therefore dictates the psychological experience of the individual. Vagal tone, or the index of functioning of the vagus nerve, particularly its influence on heart rate, has become a yardstick to evaluate stress vulnerability and emotional reactivity in humans.

Keeping the body small and tight to staunch the flow of life is a dorsal vagal survival strategy. It becomes the dominant strategy if, or when, social engagement strategies have failed because either the person's nervous system was limited in its capacity due to early life stressors that impaired the development of these ventral vagal structures, or because the levels of high sympathetic activation have exceeded the body's capacity to metabolize them.

In general, having high vagal tone and higher heart rate variability has been associated with more positive psychophysiological, behavioral, and social performance. Conversely, having low vagal tone is associated with poor health and emotional and mental health as well as interpersonal behaviors.

Additionally, research has highlighted the role of early attachment as having a significant effect on later expression of vagal tone. Children with more secure attachments exhibited greater empathetic responsiveness, less social inhibition, and higher vagal tone, emphasizing the vagus nerve's regulatory effect on emotional and social function.

Porges also coined the term neuroception, which he defines as the subconscious system that detects threat and safety, most likely at the level of the limbic brain structures. Humans need to feel safe in order to bond and befriend. If the sense of safety is impaired, the system's default is to move into sympathetic defensive responses of fight or flight, or directly to shut down if their nervous system is conditioned to do so. One could say that many psychiatric symptoms are mediated by a faulty neuroception, where the detection of threat where there is no threat, or the absence of a sense of safety, rules the person's experience. This is common in people with post-traumatic stress syndromes.

Vagal tone decreases heart rate and makes it more variable. Inhalation temporarily suppresses vagal activity, causing an immediate increase in heart rate. Exhalation then decreases heart rate as it causes vagal activity to resume.

Because breathing has such a profound effect on vagal tone and heart rate variability, it follows that breathing exercises, such as those proposed by the practice of yoga, would be a direct way to improve vagal tone. In fact, researchers have demonstrated that yoga works precisely because it tones the vagus nerve, which regulates the homeostasis, or resting state, of the majority of the body's internal organ systems that operate on a largely subconscious level, such as the heart, lungs, eyes, glands and digestive tract.

But it is not that simple. Because high sympathetic activation levels that are not regulated lead to a dorsal vagal or shut-down state, when you begin to release the dorsal break by taking in deep breaths, levels of activation or "anxiety" can increase rapidly in many individuals, boomeranging them back into shut down. It is important, therefore, to titrate this process for such individuals. In the same manner as the re-feeding process of an anorexic is titrated so the body can maintain electrolyte balance, so too does the re-entering of life energy through the breath must be titrated to the individual's window of tolerance.

Too much breath is the equivalent of too much food. They are both the intake of life in a system that has been hibernating in order to maintain life with the bare minimum of energy consumption. Rather than prescribing deep abdominal breathing at ratio of five or six second inhales with equal exhales, it might be best to suggest simply observing the breath and trying to "smooth out" the pauses until the breath flows more easily. Simple awareness of the breath might initiate increased breath regulation. When the person can tolerate observing the breath, one might invite them to make their inhales and their exhales of equal length, even if for them that is three seconds or less each until they can manage deepening and lengthening the breath.

Once the breath begins to circulate, cardiovascular rhythm also is increased. The person may begin to feel their heartbeat as well as perhaps some tingling in the skin or limbs. It is important to educate them that this is the feeling of aliveness rather than a symptom of anxiety. Because they have become conditioned to experience any elevation in heart rate as fear, it is possible that their bodies have also become accustomed to tightening and constricting in order to suppress these sensations. Gradually, the level of tolerance of these once intolerable sensations will increase, allowing the individual to be able to sustain more expansive states.

Eventually, once the capacity for even breath is in place, extending the length of exhales will become a way to soothe the mind, the emotions and the sensations by bringing carbon dioxide and oxygen levels into balance.

Journaling Exercises

1. Pause for a moment and watch your breath. How would you describe it? Is it choppy or fluid? Shallow or deep? Constricted or expansive?

   ____
   ____
   ____
   ____
   ____

2. As you notice your breath, of what else do you become aware? Are there any thoughts or judgments? Are there any emotions or images? Are there any other sensations?

    ____

    ____

    ____

    ____

    ____

3. Practice non-judgmental awareness. How does observing without interpretation impact the quality of your breath? Does it change?

    ____

    ____

    ____

    ____

    ____

4. Practice equal breathing to your most comfortable ratio. Once your inhale and exhale are approximately the same rate, continue for one to two minutes. What is your experience?

    ____

    ____

    ____

    ____

    ____

5. If you can lengthen the exhale, making it one or two seconds longer than your inhale. What begins to happen? How do you feel after this practice?

    ____

    ____

    ____

    ____

    ____

6. As you reflect on the meaning of neuroception, can you identify moments when you *know* you are safe but you do not *feel* safe?

7. Because the vagus nerve is impacted through the eyes, let your eyes explore the room around you, let them decide where to look and what they find pleasant. When you find something pleasant, let your eyes rest, feel them "drop" into their sockets and relax. Does this increase your feeling of safety?

8. Are there people in your life who help you feel safe? Bring them to your awareness. Imagine them looking at you with kind eyes. How do you begin to feel?

CHAPTER 8

Coming to our Senses: Listen to your Body to Heal

I WAS INTRODUCED TO DR. Peter Levine's work in 2005 when I was asked to read *Waking the Tiger: Healing Trauma* as part of a trauma training at the Miami Trauma Resolution Center, a publicly-funded but privately-run center dedicated to serving victims of crime such as domestic violence, sexual assault and, because Miami is a gateway city, political violence and torture in their countries of origin. The book presented a hopeful view of a human being's innate capacity to rebound from overwhelming life experiences. It also introduced me to the idea that these innate resources resided in the body and in the nervous system's intrinsic design, not only in the external world.

Given my personal history of healing through the use of body-centered modalities, I resonated with approaches that would incorporate the body in psychotherapy. When the time came to enhance my clinical training, I decided to enroll in a post-graduate training in somatic psychotherapy. In searching for a credible program, I remembered *Waking the Tiger* and decided to look into Somatic Experiencing® (SE).

There was a second program that intrigued me, and that was Pat Ogden's Sensorimotor Psychotherapy. I had also read Pat's book *Trauma and the Body: A Sensorimotor Approach to Psychotherapy*. With forewords by Daniel Siegel and Bessel van der Kolk, leading figures in the field of interpersonal neurobiology, mindfulness and trauma, I was convinced I should consider that training as an option as well.

My next step was to review the curriculum outlines for both programs, and look at overall time and cost investments. Interestingly, both training institutes were located in Boulder, Colorado, a part of the world that would become integral to my healing. The training levels and modules were similar in scope, length and cost. In the end, my heart drew me to SE and I chose to travel to Boulder for a total of thirty-six days of training over three years to complete the certificate program, which required a number of personal sessions plus consultations each year as part of the experiential portion of the learning.

In those three years of training, I learned to navigate this vehicle called my body. In a way, I obtained my "owner's manual" so I could more efficiently run and maintain the vehicle of my body-mind operating optimally. By understanding the autonomic nervous system and all of its survival phases, I learned that I did not need to be at the mercy of unnecessary and irrelevant survival responses and its accompanying chronic, unresolved, neurophysiological stress. I gained skills to expedite "resourced" or balanced autonomic states, meaning that I could observe my stress being activated by triggers in a fearless, non-judgmental fashion with the awareness of here-and-now safety and resources, which would allow that stress response to peak, discharge and resolve, returning my organism to equilibrium.

In a few words, SE allowed me to cultivate the art of observation. The stronger my capacity to witness the contents of my mind and the responses in my body, the more detached I became from the stories that had defined my identity. In short, SE is mindfulness on steroids.

Bessel van der Kolk states that "trauma is in the body, not the story."

"Traumatized individuals are prone to experience the present with physical sensations and emotions associated with the past...If past experience is embodied in current physiological states and action tendencies and the trauma is reenacted in breath, gestures, sensory perceptions, movement, emotion and thought, therapy may be most effective if it facilitates self-awareness and self-regulation." Van der

Kolk argues in a 2006 article on the clinical implications of neuroscience in the treatment of trauma.

If trauma is embodied as our sensory impressions, breathing constriction patterns, physical movements and gestures, and their associated patterns of thinking and feeling, it would make sense that mindfulness of these five things in present-moment-awareness would be the way to go to facilitate change.

"Change in the nervous system happens in the here-and-now," my SE teacher Diane Poole Heller instructed us during our first session of Beginning Level I. "We cannot go back and change history, but we can change the way our nervous system responds to that history's triggers in the present moment."

We learned the basics of autonomic nervous system functioning – sympathetic and parasympathetic responses – as well as the more current understanding of the parasympathetic nervous system as being "polyvagal," meaning that the vagus nerve, which mediates the parasympathetic response, has two branches: a ventral vagal or social engagement branch and a dorsal vagal or immobility response.

All of these autonomic responses are biologically wired for our survival, and they operate automatically when our reptilian and limbic brains interpret sensory information as a threat based on historical conditioning. For someone like me, who'd experienced trauma since I was in my mother's womb, at birth, and chronically after that, the threat response was hard-wired. Despite all the years of therapy, my nervous system was still patterned to be in sympathetic high arousal even with the slightest of stressors. This is a pattern that SE calls global high intensity activation, a pattern where oxygen deprivation sends every cell in the body into high alert. This is usually the result of pre- and peri-natal trauma, early trauma, anesthesia, suffocation, choking or drowning, all of which I had experienced.

One of the symptoms of this conditioned threat response in me was chronic neck and shoulder pain that was virtually unchanged by years of chiropractic treatment, massage therapy and acupuncture. Every time I felt stress, my neck and shoulders would begin to hurt and the pain and tension would increase until I had some manipulation and release. I had speculated, wrongly, on the original source of this pain, until an SE session revealed its source.

❧

I am sitting across from Gil on the couch of a small office with a painting of a Rocky Mountain landscape to my left, and the door to my right. Something Gil notices, maybe my eyes shifting reflexively towards the right, leads him to ask me to move my neck slowly in that direction.

"Slow it *way* down," he instructs. As I move my eyes and follow them with my neck movement, I hit a spike of fright. My breath catches in my throat with an audible gasp, and my right arm begins to grow cold, then numb.

"Okay, stop right there," he asks, guiding me to return my gaze to a picture of snow-capped mountains that I had admired earlier in the session. I had just returned from a hiking trip in Glacier National Park and told him that was one of my resources. Thinking about the engagement of my leg muscles as I trudged upward on the trail, recalling the cool air and the warmth of the sun on my skin, the sights and smells of the surrounding scenery, my fear slowly diminishes and I am able to simply allow the arm to be numb until it, almost literally, "thaws out." When I tell you it was numb, it was numb – completely anesthetized, immobile, like a lump of wet clay and icy cold. Gradually, I begin to feel pins and needles, reminiscent of a foot that's "fallen asleep" from sitting on it.

My emotional state is one of awe and curiosity. My mind is actively trying to understand what is happening and to make up a story about it – was it the car accident I was in when I was five? We were hit from the right; or was it the breast cancer surgery?

Gil asks me to hold off on figuring out a meaning until the meaning emerges organically in the form of an image or a clear memory. It does so on a subsequent session, in a subsequent training module, and it was nothing I had ever considered traumatic – when I was seven I had fallen backwards on my head and bust open my skull. The incident was coupled with shame because my brother and I had been playing we were superheroes who could fly and, running as fast as I could, I had jumped up to swing from the clothing lines in our outdoors laundry room, flipping backwards and landing hard on the cement floor on the right side of my skull and right shoulder.

During the session in which I process that fall – gradually, I might add, because the feeling of flying through the air backwards sends me into waves of nausea – I recognized the feeling of my right shoulder bracing against the impact as the exact response I had every time I felt stressed. In nervous system language, the sensory information relayed to my brain from stress – whether the stress of a deadline, or the stress of speaking in public, or the stress of "how am I going to pay the rent this month?" – was interpreted by my mid-brain as "oh, that feels exactly like that time you fell on your head." Consequently, my right shoulder went up to my ear and my arm braced for a phantom impact.

Years of chronically engaging in that response, unconsciously, had created a musculo-skeletal pattern of constriction and pain. And even though I could not alter the herniation in my cervical spine or the wear and tear of the physical body, the release of tension, and the "uncoupling," or dis-associating of the sensory information of stress with immediate shoulder bracing, reduced my pain response by about eighty percent within a few sessions.

In the Intermediate year of this three-year SE training, the focus of one of three four-day session is on interpersonal attacks and early developmental trauma. I muster the nerve to volunteer to serve as the client in a demo session conducted by the faculty. Demo sessions serve the students by demonstrating how a seasoned clinician will apply the SE principles being studied didactically. I face my biggest fear, which is sitting in front of a room of people being scrutinized and "seen" in an unembellished, vulnerable state. This pattern, in and of itself, is indicative of early developmental trauma – in my case, some blend of anxious/ambivalent and disorganized attachment.

The session was videotaped for training purposes. As I review the tape, I am struck by how little is "happening," given the intensity of my internal experience. There are very few words spoken over a forty-five minute period, but it is clear that the facilitator, Diane, is keenly attuned to my internal experience. What she sees was not clear to me until after a few years of practice. This is the beauty of SE. It is a science and an art. We learn to "see" deeply, and "listen" acutely, to the story the body is broadcasting, moment by moment, through processes as minute as pupils dilating and contracting, the pulsation of arterial veins, blinking or staring and all forms of activations in the eyes, the softness or stiffness of the body.

On this day, we are working for a while with my eyes and eye gaze, helping my body to both discharge the activation of being seen so I can properly see the gaze of another for its kind intent. We are, in fact, extinguishing the memory of critical and unloving eyes, and restoring my capacity to experience people seeing me from a present-day orientation. We gradually move from the interpersonal experience of one-to-one eye contact to the experience of seeing the entire group seeing me. After a few passes, when being seen by the group feels safer in my body, I am impacted by the compassion and love that their gazes radiate toward me. I am moved from trusting only the embrace and hold of a universal being, to trusting humanity again.

As I continued training, and subsequently working with traumatized individuals in this body-awareness fashion, I became convinced about the power of mindfully attending to sensory information to uncover implicit memories – those memories that are not encoded in the narrative databanks of the brain, but are encoded as fragmented survival responses that can be recalled by similar, albeit not exact, present-day sensory information.

Working with sensory-motor impulses, while also attending to images, emotions, thoughts and the meanings we assign to our experience, meant that I could work with pre-verbal, pre-psychological traumas that talk therapy cannot reach. Just as I had learned to understand my own autonomic responses, and how to facilitate discharge of activation and movement toward self-regulation, I could teach others to do the same – to free themselves from the shackles of the past and learn to live joyfully and fully in the here-and-now.

This was a very different paradigm from treatment when I first sought help for my childhood traumas. In the 1990s, we were still hitting pillows – what Diane humorously called "pillow abuse." I could have hit pillows until I was blue in the face and still not complete a fight response because the act of hitting those pillows was not tied to any relevant past – or current, for that matter – event. Cathartic releases, it turns out, do not seem to integrate and create lasting changes in autonomic function. They feel good in the moment because they have exhausted a surge of sympathetic activation, but the conditioned response patterns to specific and relevant triggers remain.

In the 1990s, and sadly still today, trauma work was all about the story, which we now know can be overwhelming and re-traumatize people by having them re-live horrific, overwhelming experiences. Until Bessel van der Kolk started writing about "the fragmentary nature of traumatic memories", "the limits of talk", and how "the body keeps the score", therapists were misguidedly making people talk about the story over and over, reinforcing the nervous system responses that were creating the very symptoms that brought people into therapy.

That's not to say that some people did not benefit, but many didn't, and some ran away from treatment because, on some intrinsic level, they were protecting themselves from reliving the horror. Those who benefited did so because, in the retelling, they were able to renegotiate the meaning of their experience. Those who didn't, simply did not have the autonomic capacity to re-experience the terror without the immobility response. They were caught in the trauma trap, and did not know how to access the safety available to them in the here-and-now.

"Right here, right now," I hear myself saying to myself. "Look around and see what you see." Most of the time, the stories playing in my head have no reflection whatsoever in reality. So I've become fond of saying "I suffer because of the stories I tell myself about myself."

In his book *Coming to Our Senses*, mindfulness guru Jon Kabat-Zinn, who almost single-handedly brought mindfulness to mainstream America through his work on stress reduction and pain management at the University of Massachusetts Medical School, teaches how to use our five senses – touch, hearing, sight, taste, and smell – with awareness, to become more grounded in the moment.

Grounded in the moment, I am aware of relative safety and the absence of imminent threat – no tiger jumping out of the woods to eat me, no boogie man popping from under my bed to pull me under, no falling walls or tsunami waves to suffocate or drown me. Continuously aware of this objective safety, I can explore the sensory memories that are residual from past events, enabling my body to complete any incomplete survival responses so the energy does not need to be reactivated unconsciously by current day triggers irrelevant to any life threat.

In this fashion, I processed traumatic memories that spanned decades and ranged from the womb, to birth, through infancy and throughout the lifespan – earthquakes, war, falls, surgeries, domestic violence, and various experiences of sexual molestation in my youth. My body expressed its unresolved fight, flight and freeze responses creatively to renegotiate these past events and come into the fourth "F", flow. Then, the past could remain just that: Past. I was freed to deal with present moment challenges with just the right amount of energy necessary, and with regulated, rhythmic calm when no defenses are needed.

Incorporating mindfulness and expressive practices into this somatic understanding of how my nervous operated enabled me to more easily and readily access my innate self-regulatory capacities so people began to praise me in this way: "You have a very nice nervous system." It remains the favorite compliment I've ever received.

Knowing my "owner's manual" also gave me a "dimmer switch" with which to modulate my emotional responses to fit the current situation. I became the observer of these emotional ripples on the lake of my mind, rather than the person drowning in the turbulence. This mode of autonomic self-regulation is different from imposed self-regulation through repression of emotions or stressful responses. These still happen, of course, because I am alive. If I witness a cyclist being hit by a car, or experience a near-miss auto accident myself, or someone gets angry and yells at me, my body will secrete the appropriate surge of adrenocorticotropic hormones so I can respond to the "threat." The difference is that I now know to observe it and give the body plenty of time to discharge these unnecessary hormones once the "threat" is over or deemed a "non-threat." I will allow myself to witness the tingling sensations in my nerve endings until my body will either tremble or sweat to release them and return to a natural rhythm. We are designed to be a wave of bliss.

In addition to observing and allowing, I also know to seek out social contact with a supportive individual as a way to engage my "ventral vagal system", which will downshift the threat response – not to tell them the story so we can both get activated, but simply to have them hold my hand and be with me so these sometimes intense reactions can settle in the container of our joined awareness. Silence is best, and touch is critical to support this process. A hand on a shoulder or middle of the upper back, few words (if any) and in a soft tone, or even foot-to-foot contact can go a long way to soothe even the most intolerable states of activation.

It is not until I am fifty-one that I experience a rebirth to life as a pleasurable experience. At a weekend retreat in Boulder, advanced SE faculty Steve Hoskinson helps us explore what he terms Organic Intelligence™ through the embodiment of pleasant experiences. The nervous system is a complex system, he teaches, that when in chaos will seek to organize toward control and then eventually toward coherence, if supported in a very particular way. The key, he says, is to stabilize our ability to experience the pleasant. Focusing on the traumatic, he believes, will only reinforce and increase the chaos.

This is a theory that I have been able to confirm both in myself and in my work with clients. It is not that we avoid what hurts, and what causes us suffering. It is that we begin by seeking out that which is working, that which we enjoy even if it is only in nanoseconds. On that September day of my fifty-first birthday, an age I did not think I'd reach when I was diagnosed with cancer at forty-three, it was the organic movement in my toes that, because I attend to it mindfully, sends me into full-body bliss. I feel what, as a child, I did not get to experience: the freedom to be spontaneous and express myself fully, even if I look or sound ridiculous. I laugh, I cry, I live.

Reflections

Even Freud, the father of talk therapy, said that our first sense of self is embodied, coming from the touch and holding we receive from our primary caregivers. But through the first century of modern, Western psychotherapy, this seemed to have been lost. The sense of ourselves in psychotherapy became conceptual and symbolic, rather than experiential or embodied.

Nevertheless, the body made its way back into the equation with Austrian psychoanalyst Wilhelm Reich and others who spoke of the physiological expressions of character structures, such as "body armoring," a term we can all relate to in the twenty-first century as we experience the tension of chronic stress in our bodies. He influenced Fritz Perls' Gestalt therapy, which focuses on enhanced consciousness of physical sensations, emotions, perceptions and movements in present-moment awareness.

The "decade of the brain," which by now is on its way to becoming the century of the brain, has brought forth many discoveries to support and endorse the use of mindfulness, and particularly body mindfulness, as treatment for physical and emotional ailments. Terms such as interoception have entered the nomenclature and are used by yoga teachers as readily as by neuroscientists.

Dr. A.D. "Bud" Craig, a functional neuroanatomist interested in the representation of feelings from the body, which affects theories of emotion and consciousness, has written extensively on the subject of interoception. He defines interoception as the sense of the physical condition of the body. We perceive feelings from our body, he states, that allow us to know our energy, our stress levels, our mood and our behavioral impulses. He's identified the neural structures that mediate this process of "knowing" and named the insula as the part of our brain that can help us sense and make sense of proprioceptive – the sense of the body in space – and sensorimotor – involving motor movement pathways – information arising from the body to the brain.

In a way, interoception gives us our sense of self, though it's usually below the level of consciousness unless properly stimulated. Current research into mindfulness, meditation and yoga has determined, through the use of fMRIs, that the insular and anterior cingulate cortex are "strengthened," or become thicker and more active, in those who meditate. High interoception, just as high vagal tone and heart rate variability (discussed in an earlier chapter), have been associated with greater levels of wellbeing, health and mental health. Low interoception, on the other hand, has been linked to poorer health and higher levels of psychopathology, including eating disorders.

It makes sense that people with the range of eating disorders, and more significantly anorexia, have problems with interoceptive awareness that leads them to ignore or not accurately assess hunger, fullness and satiety. Deficits in proprioceptive and kinesthetic awareness, as you might imagine, could underlie distortions in body image, which is the representation of the body in the brain. And finally, these low levels of awareness of body messages might also be at play in alexithymia, or the inability to read one's own emotions.

If we take these insights from neuroscience research seriously, it follows that we should be paying much more attention to therapies that take us beyond talk from the conceptual to the experiential. Mindfulness is not enough. Knowing what to be mindful of and what to pay less attention to, might help people integrate their experiences and develop interoceptive capacity that will lead them to full, open awareness of every experience, as it is, in the moment.

The body is key. Dr. Porges states in his book The Polyvagal Theory that eighty percent of the nerve fibers in the vagus nerve, the nerve that connects our brain and our body, are afferent nerves – meaning they carry sensory information from the body to the brain for interpretation. The remaining nerve fibers are efferent, that is, they carry information from the brain to motor fibers in the body for action. If our bodies are organized in this way, and if all cognition is therefore embodied cognition, we must consider the body as an important tool for transforming experience.

I will address here the "lack of evidence" that is blocking the integration of body oriented therapies into mainstream treatment. First of all, it must be noted that all psychotherapies once lacked evidence, and that the preponderance of the evidence is that all psychotherapies work just about equally with about fifty percent efficacy – meaning that about half of all people fail to be helped by psychotherapy – given the right conditions for the therapeutic relationship, qualities of the client and qualities of the therapist.

The levels of evidence are, first, anecdotal evidence, followed by case studies and non-experimental design studies. This evidence already exists for many body oriented therapies including yoga, SE, movement therapies and expressive therapies. Second, funding for experimental and gold-standard randomized controlled trials is extremely difficult to obtain, which dampens the possibility to establish such "evidenced-based" standards for many existing and potentially helpful therapies.

In the end, the clients who are helped are the best evidence. They often self-select out of psychiatric/medical models and treatment as usual to follow their intuition into "alternative" modalities, often with great success. Should we throw that evidence out because it is only anecdotal or single-case design?

Journaling Exercises

1. Here are a few sensation words: tight, lose, constricted, expansive, tingly, numb, cold, hot, vibrating, jumpy, tense, calm. Pause and notice which of these you are aware of in this moment. Where do you feel that sensation in your body? What happens as you observe that sensation?

 ____

 ____

 ____

 ____

 ____

2. "Good" interoceptors are able to feel their heart beating accurately without taking their pulse. Pause and notice if you can sense your heartbeat. Is it fast, or slow? Strong or weak? What happens when you observe? Does it become more apparent or less apparent?

 ____

 ____

 ____

 ____

 ____

3. Now sense your body in space. Notice where your body touches another surface. Press your feet into the ground and your back against the sofa. What happens as you notice your body? Do you feel some parts more than others? As you observe, can you get a more continuous awareness of all parts connected to one another?

 ____

 ____

 ____

 ____

 ____

4. Sit quietly and explore your world through your senses. Let your eyes see what they see, allowing them to move without directing them, letting them choose what to take in. Then switch to sound. Let your ears receive the sound and notice what sounds are available in the environment. Do this for a minute or two before switching to the sense of smell. Are there any aromas you notice or can you seek one out? As you become more aware of your environment, what happens in your experience?

____

____

____

____

____

5. Watch the contents of your mind and begin to differentiate between different categories. Notice that there are thoughts and separate from them. Observe that there may be images and create some distance from them. Pay attention to sensations and surf the waves without getting "hooked" by judgments or evaluations. Now notice the one observing. Can you be the observer of your experience without getting caught up in it? As you do that, do you notice a fluid change or do things get stuck? Keep moving back into witnessing non-judgmentally.

____

____

____

____

____

6. Become aware of your body posture. Is it slack or upright? Stand up and "act" depressed, letting your shoulders drop forward and slouch, frowning. How do you feel? Now change your posture to one of confidence, shoulders back, chest lifting up as you take in more breath, feeling your legs strongly grounded, letting the corners of your mouth softly lift into a smile. What happens to your mood as you change your posture?

   ____

   ____

   ____

   ____

   ____

7. Practice Organic Intelligence™ by focusing mostly on the positives – things that you like, things that you are good at, parts of your body that don't hurt, people who are nice and supportive to you. Only let your awareness briefly connect with the unpleasant or uncomfortable, guiding it back to positives over and over. What begins to happen to your stress, or to your pain?

   ____

   ____

   ____

   ____

   ____

CHAPTER 9

The Alchemical Power of Emotions: How Emotions Transform Your Life

ANGER WAS BEAT OUT OF me by the time I was three, when I threw a tantrum and received a beating that remains vivid. I learned not to acknowledge or express that emotion. My joy and exuberance made me a clumsy child, and the scathing looks I received from my mother soon snuffed those expressions as well. Guilt and shame became companions, and I hid in my room with my books, wrapped in their uncomfortable embrace. The main emotion I recall as a child was fear, and fear quickly escalated to terror until soon, every emotional trigger became a powder keg explosion that was hard to contain, much less process in my frail child's body.

My mother liked to party more than my father. They would go out and leave us with hired caregivers who enjoyed frightening us with scary folk tales. I waited anxiously for their return, imagining all manner of horrors that would prevent them from coming home in one piece, or ever. Invariably, my father would come home first, fuming because my mother refused to leave the party with him. Then, when Mom arrived (drunk or stoned), the fighting would begin.

"People are going to think you're a whore," my father would yell, seemingly more concerned about image than any actual felony my mother might commit.

"I just want to have fun," my mother would retort, accusing him of ruining her life.

Fighting loudly was rare. Mostly, my father expressed his anger when he was alone, throwing and breaking things in the bedroom but not taking it out on others. Once, he hurled a bottle of Methylate against the bathroom wall, leaving a blood-like stain that reminded me of the gory murder pictures published in *La Prensa* or *Novedades* newspapers. Or, we would hear them hissing at each other in English or German so we would not understand what was being said. Worse yet was the silence between them, the air cold and thick as clear gelatin, their icy stares atomic missiles of hatred.

"What's wrong?" I would ask.

"Nothing's wrong," Mom would say. "You are imagining things."

My gut told me one thing. The environment told me another. I learned to mistrust my gut. That was the beginning of the loss of an interoceptive capacity that was there in early life.

I feared my father's rage, even knowing I was safe from it. As a kid, I blamed it on my mother, not understanding the dynamics of adult relationships nor having all of the information. My childish mind believed that if only she complied with the confines imposed on her by marriage and motherhood, my father would love her, and we could all feel at peace, safe and secure in our a sense of permanency. If only she stayed at home instead of running around with her friends, leaving the maids to raise us. If only someone cared about how I felt inside and did something to help…I made myself sick with these idealized scenarios swirling through my head.

Returning from our weekend trips to the ocean, I would pray that we would make it home safely without crashing into the abyss, my father driving drunk, my mother icy next to him. I feared they would divorce. I would hold my little brother's hand and silently pray to a guardian angel I did not believe existed, "please, don't let my parents get divorced."

On one of those weekends we are in Xiloá, a lagoon that was once an extinct volcanic crater. I have eaten a dozen hard-boiled eggs, one after the other, each lathered in coarse salt. I stop only when I can't swallow a single additional bite and my stuffed tummy protrudes like a tiny burial mound. A putrid burp that smells of death escapes me. I think of the unformed chicken embryos I've just consumed and I want to puke, but I don't. Instead, I burp some more and smell the same sulfuric smell that sometimes blows from the other side of the lagoon, vestige of its volcanic origins.

"You ate every single egg," my mother yells. "What is wrong with you, *muchachita*?"

How can I answer that? At nine, I don't know what's wrong with me, but clearly something is. I feel tears sting the rim of my eyes. I try to hold them back because: a) my mother gets angrier when she sees me cry; and b) to deny her the pleasure of knowing she hurt me. She doesn't know yet that I also ate the whole bag of *meneitos* (a puffy cheese snack with no resemblance to any real food), as well as roasted chicken, *rosquillas*, and warm Coca Cola.

My father is busy pulling the boat out of the stinky lagoon and hooking it up to the car. I know he's been drinking rum with beer chasers with the other men, and my mother is nervous about his driving. I sense the tension like an electric charge in the air, not unlike the ionic discharge of lightning. The cicadas are chirping a loud song as clouds of parrots seek shelter in the trees, making a racket. My father works in silence, getting the boat on the trailer while my mother shoots arrows at him with her eyes.

My best friend Martha Margarita is with us, and I feel a flutter of embarrassment wash through me despite the massive amounts of food I have consumed to squelch the uneasiness. My body is tense, fingers flexing and curling, bitten-down fingernails cutting into the flesh of my palm as dusk settles and the sky darkens through various shades of gray.

My mother approaches my father. "Maybe I should drive; you've had a lot to drink."

He snaps at her, and refuses to hand over the keys, yelling at us to get in the car. We pile into the small Datsun, barely big enough to haul the boat. I notice my Dad's wobble, his fumbling with the keys, and tense up even more.

The car, boat in tow, jerks and jolts ahead on the dirt road, crushing rocks into pebbles in its path. Hitting the asphalt road brought no relief, as we are now on a winding road, the car swaying dangerously as my Dad swerves in and out of his lane.

The fighting is in full swing, my mother demanding that my father stop the car and hand over the keys, my father denying being drunk or impaired. Peter, Martha and I huddle in the back seat, joining my mother in a chorus: "*Papi*, please let *mami* drive." I am mortified that my friend is witnessing this event, and ashamed of what she might tell her parents, and our friends in school. I imagine her telling them, "Inge's father *es un borracho*." I don't want people to think my father is a drunk.

Our prayers answered, if not our pleas, we make it home safely. Dad sobering up mile by mile, he can walk almost straight as we unload the car. Everyone is silent, my father pensive, my mother cold in her silent scorn, Peter asleep, Martha safely dropped off at her house. I am only cold, icy inside, praying once again to a God I am not sure is anything but a fairy tale made up by the nuns at our school, "Please don't let my parents get divorced." I pray this prayer in cars, at school, on the bus, in my bed, begging God to keep my parents together. I am filled with terror at the thought of them separating, wondering where would we go, what would we do?

Divorce is not yet common in the mid-1960s, but I have learned the word and it scares me that my parents might get one. I am painfully aware there's something wrong at home, despite the frequent denials from my parents. I feel the very foundations of our existence shattering, as if from a force greater than any earthquake I had yet to feel. I am like a blind person stumbling in the dark, seeking something solid to hang on to, sensing the ground shift beneath me and give way to a nothingness and emptiness that makes the gnawing dread in my visceral cavity constrict all my organs until they are nothing but dried up chaff.

To be fair, I had plenty of reasons to be afraid. In addition to the simmering war between my parents, a movement to overthrow the family that had ruled the country for about three decades was gaining momentum.

In 1933, Anastasio "Tacho" Somoza García had been appointed head of the National Guard by departing U.S. Marines tired of waging an unsuccessful war against rebel forces led by General Augusto César Sandino. In 1934, Somoza ordered Sandino assassinated, and in 1936 staged an overthrow to get himself fraudulently elected. "Tacho" then ruled from 1936 until he was assassinated two decades later, in good Nicaraguan fashion, by a poet. Following Tacho's assassination, his son, Luis Somoza Debayle, became president and ruled until 1963, when he refused to run for reelection. His brother, head of the National Guard and soon-to-be dictator Anastasio "Tachito" Somoza Debayle, made sure politicians loyal to the Somozas ruled the country until 1967, when he was "elected" president. He would then rule (with a brief interlude) until he was ousted by the Sandinista Revolution in 1979. Tachito, like his father, was assassinated while in exile in Paraguay in 1980, when a rocket and anti-tank grenades were launched into his Mercedes Benz.

The *Frente Sandinista de Liberación Nacional* (FSLN), founded in the year of my birth by teacher-librarian Carlos Fonseca, and named after the rebel murdered by Tacho in 1936, began their attempts to overthrow the Somoza regime in 1963 when I was only two-years-old. They remained largely ineffective until 1974, when a guerrilla group seized a group of important government hostages at a party in a prominent Managua neighborhood, not far from my own. They obtained $2 million in ransom along with the release of political prisoners (including Daniel Ortega, who would become president in 1985 and again in 2007), and safe passage out of Nicaragua. After that, the war would rage on until 1979, and for years after that in the form of the *Contras* (or counter-revolutionaries supported by U.S. President Ronald Reagan) until a democratically-elected government came to power in 1990.

But in the mid-1960s, there were rumblings and riots in the streets, such as the one that broke out one Sunday night as we were driving into Managua from our beach house. It was the day that Luis Somoza Debayle, still *de facto* ruler, died of a massive heart attack in 1967. I am sure it was a night, like many other nights, when I had been praying in the car, afraid of the dark outside the windows, the treacherous winding mountain roads, the impending doom of an imagined parental divorce, only to drive into a street revolt on our way home.

The sound of gunfire pierced the night sky and rang in my six-year-old ears. The grave voice of a radio announcer, low and somber, described the accounts of the day and the scenes in the streets of Managua. My father drove defensively, attempting to avoid the rioters gathering outside and bumping up against our windows, rattling the car.

"Stay down," my father yelled, instructing us to crouch down on the floor of the back seat until we got home to avoid being hit by a stray bullet fired by police into the crowd.

"*Mami*, you too," I yelled back from behind her seat, terrified a bullet will pierce the glass and then her head, or my father's, because he needs to look out the windshield to drive.

When we get home, my parents, my grandmother, Yoya and Margarita gather around the radio. The news, the hushed conversations, are filled with stories of corruption, torture and speculation about who will gain power. General Somoza ("Tachito"), it is rumored, has been known to throw his opponents into active volcano craters to silence their voices and make them disappear.

In addition to political unrest, the ground literally shakes, often violently and always unexpectedly, as if the earth itself is raging against injustice. A land of active and dormant volcanoes that line up the Pacific coast like sentinels guarding a border, it is prone to tremors and earthquakes that cause buildings to tumble and bury people under the rubble.

Underground boiling lava and volcanic gases expand and contract the layers of earth, cracking it as easily as saltine crackers – with deadly force in 1931 and then again in 1972, and less fatally in the 1960s, when I am only a child afraid to sleep inside at night, dreading being buried alive.

The *Momotombo,* a perfect cone-shaped landmark gracing Lake Managua, erupted and buried the entire city of old León in 1610. To this day, there is an expectation that this volcano will blow its perfect cone in a massive eruption. Our farm was close to the skirts of this volcano, on the other side of Lake Managua, and sleep eluded me every time we were there, my nights filled with nightmares of lava flowing as I raced barely ahead of it to escape its singe.

These were the fears that plagued me and kept me up at night: car accidents, injuries, earthquakes, wars, divorce. Breathless, rigid, sweating and wide-eyed, I waited, alert to the possibility of danger.

By the time I am seven, insomnia and nightmares slam me nightly, leaving me ravaged and thin and puffy-eyed. I dread dusk (a dread that will haunt me well into my thirties), bringing with it a griping terror of sleep or hours of wakeful trepidation.

The first nightmare involves Santa Claus sticking me in a box and closing its four flaps, putting me in his sled and flying off into the night sky. I don't know where he is going or if he'll ever bring me back home. This is followed by nightmares in which I am chased by a big bad wolf inside a labyrinth from which I can't escape. Then I am pursued by a tyrannosaurus down a dirt road, where I get stuck in quicksand and become easy prey. Unable to move my rubbery legs, I become quarry to all sorts of monsters in the night, waking up screaming loudly, perspiring copious amounts of salty sweat until the sheets have to be changed.

The nightmares evolve as I mature, shifting from being chased to being abandoned and lost in crowded markets, on the other side of the lagoon of Xiloá, in foreign cities where people speak a language I don't understand, and I can't find my way back to my parents. In those dreams I scream only to hear my own echo in the dark. No one helps. No one comes to my rescue. The dreams would have no resolution until decades later, after years of trauma therapy, when I finally dream that I am rescued, or if lost, find my way to safety.

I can't sleep at night because I fear the nightmares. I dread bedtime. Sheets up to my neck, I stare wide-eyed at the darkness around me as I count sheep. It doesn't work. I think about the birds in my ornithology picture book in order to wipe out the scary images in my mind. If I doze off, I wake up screaming and drenched in cold sweat. This happens night after night, throughout my seventh and into my eight year of life

Hoping to assuage my fears, my parents tear down a section of my closet and break a wall between our rooms to create a doorway through which I can run freely into their bedroom. The problem is, my parents fall asleep with the TV on until a somber man's voice would sing the Nicaraguan national anthem, with its "roar of canons" and the "blood of brothers staining the earth red." Adrenalin pumping, I muster up all my courage to bolt out of bed and run screaming to their bed before the monsters I imagine are underneath my bed grab my bare feet and pull me under.

Despite the terror that plagues me, day in and day out, awake or asleep, I develop a craving for scary books and movies. It's as if I am so used to being in a state of high agitation that I need to recreate that state. I watch Dark Shadows on TV, read The Exorcist, and Stephen King becomes a constant companion despite the sleepless nights. Like a moth to the fire, I am drawn towards the things that burn me and perpetuate the familiar state of fear by now indelibly imprinted in my psyche and my nervous system. A fear I would learn to medicate with alcohol, food and drugs.

The entries on my high school diary reveal a psyche tormented by bitterness and unhappiness. My emotional life was riddled with resentments at almost everyone I came in contact with, most prominently my family and my boyfriend, but also any close friend except one whose sweet innocence made her hard to dislike. If you had told me then that I was bitter, I would have vehemently denied it. If you had asked me then if I was angry, I would have told you that I was not. Such was the level of my denial and disconnection.

"My mother told me never to hold a grudge," I would tell you, and believed it, a perfect example of how what we believe is not necessarily the truth in our practical, day-to-day experience. Many say they believe in God, or Jesus, or Buddha, but that does not mean that they are willing to practice the teachings or give up their addiction to chronic stress and worry.

That was the case with me. I may have thought of myself one way, but what I wrote reveals the truth. Diligently, I recorded the complaints of the day, summarized my consumption of a particular drink or drug, and outlined my list of grievances with the people who populated my life. Daily, or near daily, I sought to sweeten my experience with thirty-one flavors of Baskin-Robbins ice cream, to no avail.

As early as age sixteen, I swing between feelings of hope and determination and feelings of hopelessness and helplessness.

For Christmas, I write in my diary, "I am going to try to change for the best. I am going to stand up strong and be firm in my resolve. I will be free to think my own thoughts and not join in groupthink, but without feeling lonely. I need to learn to accept my aloneness."

Before New Year even arrives, the entries have already shifted to intense pessimism that I can't deny even to myself. I have decided not to go to a New Year's Eve party because "I'm probably not going to have fun anyway."

"I'm so restless," I write. "I don't know what I want or what I like. I don't know what's right or wrong. I'll probably have fun but inside I will feel empty, as I always do. For real, I've been such a pessimist lately."

The battle between my craving for solitude and my debilitating loneliness is evident throughout the pages of my adolescent musings, as is my feeling of insecurity where relationships are concerned. One day I am in love, the next day I am roiling in despair that "love sucks."

"It enrages me to need him and it makes me feel like shit," I write just before I recall taking Quaaludes with him at a concert and having fun, but the next day recording my cynicism and sarcasm toward him because I was hurt by his inattention. I hate him one minute and myself the next, playing a no-win blame game. I revile myself for being childish and needy, and scared of criticism and rejection.

I want to be accepted, but I also rile against any form of pressure. "I don't like to listen. I feel rebellious, as if I only want to listen to my own judgment and it scares the hell out of me because I might be wrong."

January brings more evidence of my ambivalence, wanting to transcend my limitations even as I feel entrapped by them. I meditate and then berate myself for not meditating enough. I write of my confusion: "I'm such a crazy person sometimes. I am hateful, without reason, out of pure selfishness. I must overcome this egoism as much as possible, even if it is a part of being human."

It's worth mentioning that January 1978 marked the turning point in the Nicaraguan civil war that led to our exile only months later. I write about watching the news and learning of the assassination of Pedro Joaquin Chamorro, and the terror I feel not knowing if my parents are okay. I comment that I feel deep emotion, but that I am being stoic and avoid the tears that threaten to erupt.

My eating disorder shows up in those pages of teenage angst as records of my attempts to exercise my thighs away, and the tallying of the pounds I've gained or lost. This preoccupation takes the place of the unprocessed emotions that tax my capacity, away from my family and my country as it goes up in flames.

I also write frequently of hangovers, as I party with increasing ferocity to blot out the pain that I pretend I don't feel. I smoke pot almost daily and avoid food when I can, only to lose control later. I chastise myself, promising once again to start meditating, eating healthy and exercising to lose weight. I fantasize about getting diet pills, starving and becoming spiritual and ethereal, as if that will purge me of the discomfort that lives in my body.

"I have been really spaced out, without eating and forgetting everything except my convoluted and crazy thoughts," I confide to the page. "I am a little crazy right now, with about fifteen cups of sherry and no food in my stomach."

By the end of my senior year in high school, I am writing about nearly overdosing on cocaine. I blame my using on frustration with getting bad grades in school, instead of blaming the bad grades in school on my using.

"I partied too much this weekend, practically sleepwalking through the hallways in school," reads one entry. "Mrs. LeBlanc failed me in English because I couldn't even write three lines. I better cut back."

The common denominator in most of the entries I read is a thread of simmering anger, bitterness and resentment, feelings that I rarely allow myself to acknowledge because I want so badly to be "good."

Because unprocessed emotion that is bottled up accumulates in the recesses of the brain and the deepest corners of the nervous system, depression is sure to develop. "Depression is the opposite of expression," is not far from the mark. Despair is a common complaint.

"I am depressed, not wanting to talk much," I write. "I'm really mad and disappointed."

By the time I reach my late twenties, the darkness deepens. Fantasies of suicide increase. I lie in bed staring at the ceiling, my mind traveling through a dark tunnel with no light at the end. The only pinprick of illumination is the fact that I have developed some faith in a spiritual reality, and the motivation to not leave a legacy of suicide to my son, who misses me and needs a healthy mom. I just can't seem to reach that ever-flickering light, in danger of being extinguished by the depression that envelopes me.

I do choose to visit a psychiatrist and accept medication, at the urging of my therapist. What do I know? I follow the recommendations and I am prescribed a tricyclic antidepressant called Tofranil, which by 1989 has already been around for more than thirty years. I don't have much faith in it because I had witnessed my aunt Irma, who took it religiously, still swing into bouts of depression that left her immobile and unwilling to leave her room, incapacitated to the point of abandoning all her responsibilities.

The side effects are many: dizziness, anxiety, tremors, insomnia, nightmares, heart palpitations, blurred vision, ringing in the ears, increased appetite, epigastric distress, constipation, dry mouth, urinary retention, nausea, tremors, changes in sexual behavior, and yes, even "increased psychiatric symptoms" -- which I do experience and I have ever increasing mood swings, crying spells, tantrums of despair. The doctor's response: increasing the medication; then changing it, again and again. In today's practice of psychiatry, he would have added one more drug after another to create a potent and toxic "drug cocktail" with little to no scientific evidence of effectiveness and much evidence of harm. I know this because more and more doctors are doing this regardless of the paucity of research to support the practice of polypharmacy.

And thus begins my up and down journey with medications. Over a period of nine years, I take Tofranil, Anafranil, Prozac, Paxil, Effexor, and Luvox (that I can remember). Fortunately, the popularity of antipsychotics has not emerged, so I am spared those agents. I am diagnosed with a major depressive disorder, eating disorders of starvation and purging, obsessive compulsive disorder, generalized anxiety disorder, and post-traumatic stress disorder resulting from early childhood trauma compounded by the trauma of living through earthquakes, civil war and forced exile. And yet, I continue to suffer because my emotions have yet to find an outlet.

Reflections

While I was a highly emotional individual, I lacked emotional awareness, communication and processing skills. The information and wisdom inherent in emotions was not available to my conscious mind. Emotions for me where so highly charged that all I could do to survive was to vent them inappropriately or stuff them unskillfully. I did not exactly "manage" them, but even the idea of "managing" emotions conflicts with the true nature of emotion regulation, which is an autonomic function of a fully developed central nervous system that has been adequately supported to experience the adaptive function of emotions.

There is a robust body of literature showing that individuals with eating disorders experience difficulties identifying and describing emotions. Research shows that alexithymia, which basically means having no words for emotions, has been linked to emotional eating in all eating disorder subtypes and may be unaffected by clinical improvement (such as weight restoration) unless the expression of emotions is offered in treatment. Those with greater degrees of alexithymia may be more likely to channel feelings into body image distortion and obsessive-compulsive behaviors.

Alexithymia, whose features also include a paucity of imagination and an externally-oriented cognitive style, has been linked to early attachment trauma, since our earliest patterns of behavior are largely composed of implicit and non-verbal sensory-driven responses.

Given these affect-related difficulties, it is important that eating disorder treatment protocols also incorporate a focus on emotions and emotion regulation.

Feelings are mental experiences of body states and have two components: interoception and expression. The brain interprets physical states arising from the body's responses to external stimuli. They signify physiological need (for example, hunger), tissue injury (for example, pain), optimal function (for example, well-being), threats to the organism (for example, fear or anger) or specific social interactions (for example, compassion, gratitude or love). Feelings constitute a crucial component of the mechanisms of life regulation, from simple to complex. Action follows feelings, whether we are conscious of it or not.

Emotions themselves have survival functions, or evolution would have eliminated them long ago. Fear alerts us to danger and helps us to run away. Anger mobilizes energy toward defensive responses and allows us to set healthy boundaries and use our voice. Love stimulates and rewards the bonding process. Disgust insures we avoid poisonous toxins. Joy and excitement connect us to the energy and vitality available for a boundless life. Curiosity and novelty-seeking help us discover new and helpful things. Shame promotes pro-social behavior so we are not cast out from the group, which could threaten our survival. Guilt makes us repair damaged bonds so we can return to the fold.

If we listen to the message of the emotion, and are able to utilize their metabolic energy to complete the required task, our emotions naturally regulate. If we ignore or avoid the message, it will make repeated attempts, biologically that is, to communicate to us until we listen. This bound-up, unused energy circulates randomly throughout the various channels of our body-mind system, wreaking havoc with endocrine and hormone metabolism. Initially, we may call it anxiety. After we've been depleted and our system shuts down, we might call it depression. As the expression says, what we resist, persists. What we allow, simply comes and goes, like the tides.

Most mental health disorders are attributed to difficulties in the emotion regulation system. Anxiety and depression, in particular, are associated with emotional avoidance. When we negatively evaluate an emotional experience, we are more prone to shut it down. When we simply allow the experience to wash through like a wave crashing on a shore that eventually retreats back into the vast ocean, our autonomic nervous system is able to return to a homeostatic balance and we reengage with life.

Most of the time, we want to avoid pain. Paradoxically, this creates suffering. Disconnected from these powerful energies, we disconnect also from their pleasant and positive aspects, such as joy, love, vibrancy, and aliveness. Remember, pain happens, it is a necessary part of living. Pain is useful information when you touch a hot stove and move your hand to avoid the pain of a burn. But pain cannot always be avoided, particularly emotional pain. When someone we love dies, the pain of loss is intense. Suffering is refusing to accept pain. Pain can be difficult to bear, but suffering is even more difficult, because it can last forever; whereas pain, at least in its acute phase, is time-limited. Life can be worth living, even when there is pain.

Dialectical Behavior Therapy (DBT) suggests becoming mindful of a current emotion so you can respond according to the correct stimulus and not to the "faulty neuroception" we've discussed in previous chapters. Notice what's going on, externally and internally, so you can label various elements of your experience. When the emotional charge is manageable, you can observe the wave of the emotion without getting caught up in it or need to turn to self-destructive behaviors to manage. If the emotional charge is too high, DBT recommends distracting from the emotion or acting opposite of the emotion. For example, if you're angry enough to yell obscenities at your boss and this could lose you your job, leave the room and take a walk around the block until you are calmer and can speak skillfully and coherently, so you can maintain your self-respect and also your job.

DBT also proposes that individuals "cope ahead" by identifying and preparing for those people, places or situations that elicit powerful emotions. Coping ahead means that you can create and practice a plan for how you will respond in that situation as well as how you will minimize your vulnerability to emotions with self-care and through building positive experiences whenever possible.

Ultimately, emotions hold important information for us and help us communicate to others. Understanding their function, being able to recognize them when they appear, and having the skills to utilize the energy they mobilize in the appropriate dose, is the antidote to the alexithymia so common in eating disorders.

Journaling Exercises

1. What are some ways in which you avoid experiencing your emotions? What are the consequences of this avoidance? Does it cause you to feel anxious or depressed?

   ____

2. What are some emotions you enjoy having? What are some emotions you will do anything to avoid?

   ____

3. What are some of the ways you express your emotions? Are these adaptive or maladaptive?

   ____

4. When you feel angry, how do you notice it in your body? What thoughts, feelings, sensations and urges do you notice when you experience anger (include annoyance, frustration, and irritation)?

   ____

5. When you feel sad, how do you notice it in your body? What thoughts, feelings, sensations and urges do you notice when you experience sadness (include melancholy, wistfulness, and mournful)?

____

____

____

____

____

6. When you feel afraid, how do you notice it in your body? What thoughts, feelings, sensations and urges do you notice when you experience fear (include fretting, anxious, tense, agitated, timid, and stressed)?

____

____

____

____

____

7. When you feel happy, how do you notice it in your body? What thoughts, feelings, sensations and urges do you notice when you experience happiness (include joy, excitement, curiosity, enthusiasm, and elation)?

____

____

____

____

____

8. When you feel disgusted, how do you notice it in your body? What thoughts, feelings, sensations and urges do you notice when you experience disgust (include repelled, repulsed, and revolted)?

____

____

____

____

____

9. When you feel ashamed, how do you notice it in your body? What thoughts, feelings, sensations and urges do you notice when you experience shame (include embarrassment, humiliation, and rejection)?

____

____

____

____

____

10. When you feel proud, how do you notice it in your body? What thoughts, feelings, sensations and urges do you notice when you experience pride (include confidence, esteem, dignity and satisfaction)?

____

____

____

____

____

CHAPTER 10

Feeding the Hungry Heart: Recognizing what Hunger Signals

MY FIRST EXPERIENCE WITH SATISFACTION comes in the sweetness of my great-grandmother's ample bosom, her busy kitchen, and the sweets it produced. For the first three years of my life we live with her, my father's German grandmother, Elsa Lüedeking Bunge. She came to Nicaragua from Hamburg after the First World War because her husband was killed in the war and her husband's brother, known to my father as Opapa but deceased by the time I came along, lived in Nicaragua. They settled in *Casa Colorada,* near *Las Nubes* because of the cool weather, which is cool enough for strawberries and coffee trees and orchids that Omama tells me bloom only on my birthday. This delights me and causes me suspicion because I do not believe, even though I want to, that I am that special. That this flower knows to open up on the very day that marks my birth seems implausible.

Omama's house is large. We live in an apartment with a separate entrance that links to her house through a hallway. In the back, there is another house, occupied by the Heilemann's, who are our distant relatives. The youngest of the boys, Jens, is eight, five years older than I am. He and I fight for the crop of wild strawberries that grow in the front yard, hidden in a circumference of other shrubs and flowers.

The air is crisp as I step outside, glancing about me for Jens or anyone who might foil my quest. The urgency energizes my three-year-old legs, which are bare and erupting with goose bumps from the cold air in this mountain enclave outside Managua where we have lived since my birth. The distance to the strawberry patch is not great – for an adult. For me, it is fraught with danger and demanding of great courage.

I peek around the corner and run as fast as my wobbly legs will allow, safe only when I part the bushes that surround the patch and I can hide behind them. Then I begin to scavenge, picking first the reddest, sweetest berries and then – because it's been explained to me that you shouldn't pick unripe fruit – the still mostly green ones that taste more tart than sweet. I like the prickly texture, the crunchiness of the greener fruit, the little seeds that get stuck between my baby teeth.

I eat any and every strawberry I find, knowing I will get in trouble, a sickish feeling enveloping me as I imagine Omama's disappointment and the wrath of Jens who competes with me for these treats and hence inspired my early morning stealth mission. The sweet tartness of the juicy red fruit is all the more pleasurable because it is forbidden. I will develop a taste for tartness and the forbidden for the sheer pleasure of rebelling against demands imposed by culture and society.

Jens is taller, faster, and stronger, forced to share his pickings with me because he is a boy and I am a) younger and b) a girl. I can tell he resents me. Even at three I understand and can't blame him. It doesn't seem fair. We are both equally hungry, and equally insatiable. I don't want Jens to pick my berries. I want to pick my own, and I want more than he would allot me. I don't want to share mine with him either.

Eventually, our ongoing warfare decimates the strawberry patches and we no longer have something to fight over. Without strawberries, we have little in common, our age and gender differences a barrier to common enjoyment, so I return to the hearth of Omama's kitchen.

Omama's lap offers the warmth and comfort I crave, her welcoming arms representing the archetypal nurturing mother I long to have. She calls me *meine puppe* (my little doll), and teaches me my first words in German, a language I will later forget and never master. But I always comprehend the language of love expressed in her gaze, her touch, her words, and her actions.

Her warmth and sweetness is most evident in her kitchen, where she supervises a posse of cooks who roll buttery dough, beat egg whites with mountains of fine sugar, slice apples and cover them with a shower of cinnamon, and bake cookies with shaved lemon rinds. The double kitchen is separated by a dividing counter, which I occupy to listen to the cacophony of sounds, watch the dance of aproned ladies, and taste the exotic flavors concocted with both locally-grown and European flavors imported from Germany. Her kitchen overflows with sugar: refined, brown, powdered, and coarse. In liquid form: syrupy molasses, evaporated cane juice, and clear corn syrup. In this sweet drama, I eat sugar by the spoonful, mixed with butter and flour into dough, caramelized warm into *dulce de leche*, whipped into egg whites as *espumillas*, or in syrups with vanilla extract.

I am never as hungry, or lonely, or empty, or numb, in Omama's kitchen as I am on our side of the house, where I can cry in my crib until I am choking in my own salty sobs, hungry, wet, soiled, unable to breathe, because mom does not want to "spoil" me by giving in to my every need. I am left craving the milky, sweet, fatty substances that represent my great-grandmother's love, and the salt of my tears leave me with a propensity to also crave salt.

My father disappears by day and reappears at night, dressed impeccably in white, starched, short-sleeved shirts that smell of Fab detergent and sunshine. When I hear his car drive up, I run to greet him at the door, sometimes with a strawberry pie in hand. He sweeps me up and I eagerly await the verdict. Even at that young age, I remember feeling insecure about the lumpy pie crust, aware that it did not look or taste like Omama's. I find it hard to believe that he would like it as much as he likes hers.

My brother is born when I am two, and lingers near death in the hospital of a deadly pneumonia. My parents are staying with him in hospital most nights, and I am left in the care of others. I don't recall much of this experience except for a subtle sense of dread that seemed to envelop me like a soft blanket and stay with me for years, only to be built upon by future frightening experiences. He finally comes home after two months, and I love him, tending to him as if he were a little doll.

Only Omama's pastries, and her sweetness, satisfy my hunger, my longing, my fear, my growing sense of inadequacy—and only for a short period of time. The crumbling-in-your-mouth lemon-butter cookies, the raisin buttermilk pound cakes, the *dulce blanco* with cassis syrup, the *apfelstrudel* with powdered white sugar coating the top crust, and the *pfeffernüsse* biscuits fill me, however temporarily.

Gradually, over time, I become more and more alienated from my enjoyment of food. At seven I develop serious food allergies and soon food becomes the enemy. We are not sure what triggers my violent full-body hives. Is it strawberries? Is it eggs? Or is it ham? Pretty soon anything I eat is potentially threatening. I become more and more emaciated and simultaneously develop insomnia and night terrors, which leaves me gaunt and dark-eyed.

To solve the problem my mother begins to pump me full of appetite enhancers and I become ravenous, so by the time I am nine, I have filled up again. I can voraciously eat up to eight sandwiches, unaware of the effect they are having on my digestive system. I don't feel full. My stomach does not seem to expand to exploding. Until the weight creeps up, and I begin to develop curves, and with them, unexpected sensual desires. At twelve, I go on my first diet. I learn to "fast" and avoid full food groups. By thirteen, I begin to binge and purge, committed to keeping my weight below ninety-five.

Food and hunger, desire and deprivation, dread and delight, become hopelessly intertwined for me. I want to eat, to enjoy what life has to offer with passionate abandon, to satisfy my emotional needs with the sweetness of pastries like the ones in Omama's kitchen. Concurrently, I am afraid to eat, wishing to disappear, to become lighter, and to deny my need for pleasure because the shame that accompanies the longing for love, connection and satisfaction is so intense. I did not overeat because I was hungry, I overate because of some inner craving to "feed" or soothe my insatiable emotional self. I did not like to feel full because I did not know how to recognize satiety. I did not know the meaning of "enough" for many years to come.

Reflections

When I ask my clients why they are overeating, binge eating or simply misusing food, here are just a few of the answers I receive:

Boredom. Boredom is a symptom of unfed curiosity. We might be craving novelty, or our intellects may desire stimulation. Instead of reaching for a book, going to a museum or learning a new skill, we may reach for "interesting" and tasty foods to entertain us. Those with anorexia might pass the time by obsessing about food content or calorie-counting.

Loneliness. Contact nutrition is as important as physiological nutrition. We are social beings designed to be in connection with one another. This emotion is alerting us that we need to establish deeper or more meaningful relationships than the ones we are currently engaged in. Or perhaps it is indicating that we are isolating more than is proper for our personality, like a tank of gas that is too empty.

Anger. This emotion is alerting us that someone has crossed our boundaries. The physiological sensations of anger are meant to stimulate energy in our limbs and vocal cords so we can "stand up for ourselves" and "speak up." If we ignore this emotion and instead stuff it down with food, we will continue to feel victimized by others. Interestingly, people who eat over their anger tend to pick crunchy foods because clenching the jaw is part of the aggression response. Those with anorexia may reject what is offered as a way to express anger, and purging is one of the clearest metaphors for explosive rage.

Are you eating, or rejecting food, because you are lonely or sad, angry or bored? Are you eating or obsessing about your weight because your life lacks meaning and purpose? We have relational, recreational, emotional and spiritual needs that must be met for us to feel satisfied and not resort to food to avoid or ignore those needs. For example, if sad, lonely or bored, you may want to eat soft, pleasurable, filling or sweet foods. If experiencing anger, guilt or shame, you may want to ignore your body's needs and even to starve yourself, or conversely, you may crave salty or crunchy foods in excess.

In order to learn to intuitively eat and to meet our actual nutrient needs, as opposed to feeding emotional, intellectual or spiritual needs with food, we must first recognize our current patterns of eating mindless of our biological hunger, fullness and satiety cues.

Step one would require mindfulness of hunger cues. You may become aware that you start having thoughts about food or your next meal, but your body is not yet signaling strong hunger pangs. Maybe there is a mild rumbling in your stomach. You can wait to eat, but you probably don't want to wait too long. It is best to eat before you are ravenously hungry to the point that everything sounds good and you could eat anything to stop the hunger pangs, or possibly a headache, dizziness, weakness, trouble concentration, or cold sweats, all signs of low blood sugar.

Step two calls for awareness of fullness cues. Eat when you are mild to moderately hungry and can still choose what and how much you'll eat, and then check in with yourself throughout the meal to assess signals of fullness. Are you filling up but could comfortably eat some more? Continue. The key is to eat enough so you do not feel hungry again for about four hours. Eat until the hunger is gone, but also track how soon after you begin to notice hunger. Those who have lost adequate interoceptive capacity may feel the hunger is gone after only a few bites, but then realize one hour later that they are hungry again. This is a sign that you need to eat more of the right kinds of foods to satisfy hunger.

Step three means that, once full, you check in to see if you feel satisfied. Satiety is more than the feeling of fullness. You can fill up on a single food, for example a big bowl of popcorn, but you may not feel satisfied because your brain needs to receive the message that your body is receiving all necessary nutrients. It is not uncommon for people to remain "hungry" despite fullness because of this lack of nutrients in an age when we eat so many packaged foods or limit ourselves by following the latest fad diet. One easy way to make sure you are getting enough nutrients is to eat fresh foods in a variety of different colors and using satisfying spices. In Ayurvedic medicine, it is recommended that your meal have all six major tastes: sweet, salty, sour, bitter, astringent and pungent. Once we develop interoceptive ability to track our needs and the intuition to know which foods will provide it, the process of making the right choices becomes less mysterious.

Intuitive eating can be learned, but it demands deep awareness and self-inquiry. In their book, *Intuitive Eating*, registered dietitians Evelyn Tribole and Elyse Resch provide guidelines for intuitive eating. They key to intuitive eating isn't just to make peace with food, stop dieting and eat what you crave. You can eat what you crave as long as you respect your fullness, honor your body's health and find ways to deal with your emotions without using food to cover them up or avoid them.

Differentiating between physical hunger and emotional, relational, intellectual or spiritual hunger requires a lot of mindfulness and conscious awareness of your interior life, but it can be done. It is a process of trial and error, of learning and making mistakes, and best done with the guidance and support of peers and, if necessary, professionals who espouse a philosophy of eating and healing that matches yours. They key is to forgive yourself for your mistakes, radically accept your needs, and persevere in spite of failure.

Journaling Exercises

1. How do you know if you are hungry and what you are hungry for? The hungry mind generally plans how to obtain food, or daydreams about a desired food. It may also feel scattered and unable to concentrate, watching the clock for lunch or dinner time.

   ____

   ____

   ____

   ____

   ____

2. How do you know when you are full or satisfied? The comfortably full mind feels satiated and able to focus on the tasks at hand.

   ____

   ____

   ____

   ____

   ____

3. Do you chronically diet or pursue the latest fads, categorizing foods as "good" or "bad" and obsessing about your appearance? What might draw your attention if you distracted from these obsessive thoughts?

   ____

   ____

   ____

   ____

   ____

4. Do you eat primarily out of emotional rather than physical hunger? Are you aware of which emotions you are eating over? Refer to previous chapter and find a strategy to learn from, express or regulate that emotion.

____

____

____

____

____

5. Are you multitasking while you mindlessly eat a meal or snack, only to realize later that you overate? What might happen if when eating, you just eat?

____

____

____

____

____

6. When you feel hungry, how do you become aware of that in your body? What sensations do you notice when you feel hunger? What thoughts, feelings and impulses do you notice when you are aware of the sensations of hunger?

____

____

____

____

____

7. When you feel full, how do you notice that in your body? What sensations arise when you feel full? What thoughts, feelings and impulses do you notice when you notice the sensations of fullness?

   ____

   ____

   ____

   ____

   ____

8. When you feel satisfied by food, how do you notice that in your body? What sensations arise when you feel satisfied? What are the thoughts, feelings and impulses that come up when you are aware of feeling satiated by a good meal?

   ____

   ____

   ____

   ____

   ____

9. What are you truly hungry for? Can you take steps to satisfy that hunger, whether it's emotional, interpersonal, intellectual, or spiritual?

   ____

   ____

   ____

   ____

   ____

10. List the obstacles that arise in your mind to actually feeding your hungry heart with what it actually needs. Are they truly valid? Do you see a way to overcome the obstacle?

____

____

____

____

____

CHAPTER 11

Creating a Recovery Vision: Choosing a Values-Driven Life

Spirit: *1: an animating or vital principle held to give life to physical organisms; 2: a supernatural being or essence; 3: the immaterial intelligent or sentient part of a person; 4: the liquid containing ethanol and water that is distilled from an alcoholic liquid.*

IN ADDITION TO DRINKING, DRUGS, obsessions, and eating, another way I escaped the uncomfortable nature of my emotional and bodily experience was by attempting a "spiritual bypass," a term that describes the use of spiritual beliefs to bypass painful feelings.

If I could "return" to the world of the spirit I would no longer need to live in the "vale of tears" that I experienced my life to be, despite the evidence of much privilege. I pursued spiritual experiences as a bridge to another world, one where I was ethereal and did not need to feel my need, my lust, my hunger, my rage, and my desperate and unfulfilled longing for connection.

I learn about Adam and Eve in kindergarten. The story arouses curiosity me – a man created in the image of God, a woman made from his rib, both naked in paradise. I vividly imagine them walking around, naked but for a leaf covering their genitalia, eating ripe fruit – possibly juicy, fleshy mangoes or ripe papayas that I love so much – and playing with lions as if they were kittens, for they had *dominion* over everything. In other words, they were all powerful. But evil Eve had to go and eat an apple, from the Tree of Knowledge of Good and Evil no less. And why? Because a snake told her to do it. Talking snakes, even one representing the devil, was a novel idea.

"What's wrong with wanting to know the difference between good and evil?" I ask the nun, whose heavy white linen habit must have suffocated her in the steamy tropical heat. At five, I'm sure I'd rather be walking around with only a leaf for clothing, like Eve, eating fruit straight from a tree, seeking knowledge. I am a curious child, always wanting to know everything, so I'm worried about the nature of this crime that would get Eve expelled from paradise.

The nun explains to us that Eve's sin was disobedience, a concept I can't quite comprehend because I am still convinced that wanting to know the difference between good and evil is a good thing.

"She disobeyed God's order to stay away from the tree, and this brought the wrath of God upon Eve, and Adam by default, because he ate the apple too," the nun goes on, "so they were kicked out of Paradise and then they had to feel pain and suffer."

That's a harsh God, I think. And they were ashamed to be naked, on top of it. These were the sixties and my parents were known to go naked from time to time. I had been taught to consider this natural.

Because we were also taught to "discern" between right and wrong, or good and bad –and to choose to do the right thing—I ask again.

"Because they wanted to be like God, and that's not okay," the nun answers, her impatience growing.

I am still baffled, but the implications about disobedience are clear. Disobedience – of God, of our teachers, of our parents – will be met with harsh penalties.

When I get home, my mother is preparing to go out. She sits half-naked (like Eve), in front of her vanity, applying mascara.

"*Mami*, why was it wrong that Eve ate the apple from the tree of the knowledge of good and evil?"

"Don't believe everything those nuns tell you," she answers, dismissing any further conversation. Now I'm even more disconcerted. If I'm not to believe the nuns, why am I going to a Catholic school? What did the nuns ever do that they're not to be believed?

Being five, I don't yet understand the meaning of metaphors or the cultural context of biblical documents. But I know I long for knowledge. I *would* eat from the tree of knowledge. Will I be banished to the "valley of the shadow of death"? Plus, I am a woman (or will be someday), and in this story, women are shameful and blamed for the ills of men.

"How do you know it is God talking to you? Does He whisper in your ear?" I ask Sister Rina when I am in fifth grade. She's aware of my insolence, but she does more than my mother. She tries to answer my question with seriousness. Even though it's part of her job and her calling as a nun, not every nun I'd met had her level of patience and willingness to teach.

"You have to learn to listen with spiritual ears," she replies.

Still confused, feeling like I am walking in dangerous territory and resigned that my mother and the nuns will not offer any further explanation, I accept her verdict and become suspicious of everything I learn from the nuns. I become cynical of religious instruction and throughout my elementary and high school Catholic school education, I ask the nuns uncomfortable questions that get me in trouble. This defining experience led me to have a foundation for thinking critically and evaluating spiritual knowledge before accepting it as gospel.

I become even more irreverent as I grow older. By the time I reach thirteen, the excruciating emotional pain that I feel, as incomprehensible as it is, leads me to search for religious and spiritual comfort – walking to Sunday Mass by myself because my family does not attend, joining an evangelical Bible study and prayer group for adolescents, learning transcendental meditation.

We live in Las Colinas when a disciple of the Maharishi Mahesh Yogi visits Nicaragua to teach transcendental meditation. Attending Bible study and boisterous Pentecostal worship circles has not alleviated my emptiness and dysphoria. My boyfriend has given me a beautiful leather-bound Bible with the words "Inge, Daughter of God" etched in the flap. At evangelical groups loud with song, people "speak in tongues" and faint when they are "slain by the holy spirit." I try to get into the frenzy and experience something mystical, anything that will take me out of my bodily experience and rocket me into another dimension, but nothing happens other than I get a sore throat from singing so loudly.

My parents, then in their progressive phase, take me to meet this foreign guru so I can be granted my own, unique, personal mantra.

As dusk settles, we arrive at the home of Omar D'Leon, renowned artist and my mother's friend, mentor and teacher. The skies are darkening and myriad crickets burst out in song. An atmosphere of reverence envelopes everyone as they their turn to enter the makeshift sanctuary in one of Omar's back rooms. I sit outside by the pool, surrounded by Omar's lush tropical garden. A warm breeze caresses my skin, drying beads of perspiration provoked by humidity or nerves. The scent of honeysuckle, or night jasmine, tickles my nose. I am in a state of heightened awareness.

Thinking of the avocados, zapotes (a red-fleshed, avocado-like fruit), tangerines and little apricots he grows, my stomach grumbles. I am hungry, but I don't dare interrupt the adults who leave the room pensive, head down, silently shuffling to find a quiet place to reflect. I am aware of my youth and feel a combination of pride and dread. I am the only child, barely thirteen, not quite sure of the implications of this "initiation."

Finally, my turn arrives. I walk through a curtain into a darkened room redolent of linseed oil and turpentine. He is tall, dark, and has a mop of unruly, brittle hair framing a face with a wide nose and bright white teeth that appear to glow in the dark. I fidget, look down at my sandaled feet, not knowing how I am to behave in front of *Señor Guru* to demonstrate my worthiness to receive his teaching. He seems so *normal*, so *human*; he doesn't have a halo, or an *aura* of holiness. He is definitely not Hindu, nor does he wear white robes.

My field of vision feels narrow, either by the shadows of dusk, the low yellow lighting, or my nervous agitation. I recall his large hands doing something resembling a blessing, his *mala* beads, and the basic instruction of repeating the mantra over and over in my mind while seating in a semi-lotus position, nothing more extraordinary than that.

I begin to practice, and to seek esoteric knowledge by borrowing my mother's books – Wisdom of the Mystic Masters, The Third Eye, lots of books on reincarnation, out-of-body travel and more. The sense that there is no such thing as too much of a good thing seems to drive me. On a day like any other day, I decide it's time not only to meditate, but to do some breathing exercises to "counterbalance a negative condition" because melancholia feels more and more like my natural state. While my grandmother watches *telenovelas*, I escape to a reclining chair with Wisdom of the Mystic Masters, chapter one, "attaining harmonium."

I follow the instructions for counterbalancing the negative – joining index and middle fingers with thumb, counting and holding breaths (holding the inhale to the count of seven, releasing and repeating that seven times). Then, to make sure I don't become overly positive, I follow the instructions to counterbalance the positive – feet on the floor, hands in prayer position at the chest, all fingers touching to unite right and left, and again counting and holding breaths (exhaling and holding for five, and repeating the entire procedure five times). Finally, I meditate for thirty minutes while repeating the mantra I was taught, the primordial sound of creation.

When I finish, my body is lightly tingling. It feels ethereal and weightless. This feeling is more pleasurable than I had anticipated. I hear the chatter of the television and it jars me. I cannot bear to connect with material reality, so I go out into the backyard to commune with nature. My mother, an avid gardener, has planted an indubitable paradise of trees, shrubs and flowers. There are guavas, grapes, and *mimbres,* a very sour fruit I enjoyed eating with salt. I feel as if I am walking in a genuine Garden of Eden, complete with the ménage of animals my brother has collected – Urus the spider monkey, two white roosters, and a caged wild tiger from the Atlantic Coast jungles, among others.

In the back, my mother has a colorful cottage that serves as her art studio. I try to sit on its porch, but I can't. The cement feels "too man-made." I crave to merge with nature, so I glide slowly around the yard, feeling every pebble under my feet, the softness of ground cover, smelling the flowers, touching the leaves.

I begin to "see" or sense God in every leaf – a shining light flowing through the veins as the leaf *breathes,* the image of a Himalayan sage with long black hair reflected on the pulsating green. I feel the entire universe is present in each leaf, and so am I, and yet, the universe and the leaves are also present in me. The fabric that separates us is thin, filmy, translucent and permeable.

This overwhelms me and I begin to perspire. I am unsettled by this losing of a sense of self, the "I" called Inge, born in 1961 in Managua, Nicaragua. "I" am no longer a separate entity. I quake a little, even as the leaves also quiver in the breeze. I feel a sense of bliss (with a capital B), and I want to hold on to it forever. I never want to return to the house, where the TV still blares a Mexican soap opera's tragic and mournful tale. In the words of St. John of the Cross in his opus magnum, Dark Night of the Soul, *"I abandoned and forgot myself, laying my face on my Beloved; all things ceased; I went out from myself, leaving my cares forgotten among the lilies."*

And yet, I feel the pull of the "I." The voices in my head begin to argue: "You can't stay out here forever; what are people going to think?" So I tear myself away from the bliss, which still exerts a magnetic pull, feeling myself become denser and heavier with every difficult step I take back toward the house. The experience of unity and oneness slowly evaporates as I get closer to the back door – a cage-like, iron-bar door painted blue.

My grandmother tears her gaze away from the TV and glances at me, asking me what I am doing.

"Nothing," I reply.

She invites me to watch the *telenovela* with her and have a snack. I do, feeling only half there and wondering if I'll ever recapture such a state of bliss again. I am sad, slipping naturally into the familiar melancholic detachment, dissociating into the drone of the black and white TV, snared by the sad story of a maid who falls in love with her rich *patrón*.

My body becomes denser and heavier. I am aware of its blooming and blossoming and curving in ways I find uncomfortable, desiring pleasure in ways I am unprepared for. I yearn to return to the unexplainable state of bliss, but I have no one to guide me. Alcohol and drugs and starvation and purging and sex soothe me more quickly than sitting down to meditate, which may or may not have the desired effect. Spiritual ideas take a back burner and slowly slip away.

❧

Like most Americans, my idea of yoga was *asana*, or physical postures, particularly postures that required me to have incredible strength and flexibility. On the one hand, I considered yoga a wimpy form of exercise that I did not have time for when I was engaged in a war against my flesh through excessive running and aerobics. On the other hand, it was a challenging set of stretches designed to help me twist myself into an acrobatic pretzel, which was something I could not do to save my life without torqueing my vertebra painfully or tearing a ligament somewhere.

I could not, for example, stand on my head. Every time I tried I trembled and broke out in profuse sweat. The posture flooded me with a profound sense of fear that would cause my body to wobble and ultimately fall. I would kick my feet up against the wall, and quickly come down because I could not tolerate the feeling of being upside down. I also could not do fish pose, *matsyasana*, without becoming extremely nauseous.

Really, any pose that asked me to extend my upper chest up and out caused me great discomfort as implicit memories kicked in and my body recalled being upside down during the traumatic fall I had at seven when I landed backwards on the right side of my skull. Intense twists that squeezed all the toxins out of my taxed liver also were difficult. In Ayurveda as in Chinese medicine, the liver is the center of anger, and mine had been filled with unresolved anger and bitterness for most of my life. Kidneys hold our ear, and mine were flooded with it.

"You were abusing your kidneys!" an Iyengar yoga instructor once admonished me after a supported pose caused a severe detox reaction – profuse sweating, nausea and an attack of diarrhea. Uncertain about the safety of her instructions, I did not return to her class.

Another attempt at yoga left me suffering with De Quervain's tendonitis, a painful hand tendon injury that causes pain along the base of the thumb and wrist. Why? Because the asana teacher had a class of beginners moving into crane pose, *bakasana*. I had never had much upper body strength, and arm balances were still nearly impossible. But my nature (*pitta*, in Ayurvedic terms) is to try, to exert too much effort, to push beyond my limits in the service of an egoic goal. And I hurt myself. That injury took months to completely heal.

Still, I kept going to yoga. First, because I thought it would be a good way to stretch my hamstrings and quads, which were constantly tight and aching from running. Second, because there was something happening in corpse pose, *savasana*, which would become a favorite pose once I realized how much rest I needed. For just a few moments, I could completely let go. I could let the earth support me and release all effort.

I could give myself the gift of relaxation because I had "earned" it after exerting effort in the other asanas. Lastly, I knew this was supposed to be a spiritual practice, and I was on a spiritual journey. I accepted, on faith, that pranayama would help me meditate, and I had a strong desire to be a "good meditator."

Despite my perseverance, I struggled to embrace yoga, and what yoga had to offer – mainly because I did not *really* know what yoga had to offer beyond some good stretches and relaxation. And so yoga and I had an intermittent love affair. I would visit a yoga class once in a while through the years, because a friend of mine invited me, or out of curiosity. I even wrote a telling brief essay for a writing class:

> *"The yoga mat is sticky under my bare feet, a rectangle of purple rubber. I spread my toes wide and ground my feet flat on the mat as I am instructed, feeling everything, every millimeter of skin on rubber beginning to slide on a trickle of perspiration. The yoga mat is the center of the universe for that hour of practice (a practice toward spiritual enlightenment? A practice toward the integration of body, mind and spirit?)*
>
> *Grounded in the asanas and anchored in the breath, I flow through the postures as energy rises from my core like a furnace heating a house. My breath becomes labored and I struggle to keep it flowing. Sweat beads begin to form on my face, first on my upper lip (I lick them off, salty) and then on my brow, where they eventually slide into my eyes, stinging like hot tears. This is not strenuous, I think. Not like running 20 miles training for a marathon. Yet my body is heating up, everywhere, as we do forward bends, back bends, triangle and reverse triangle poses.*
>
> *We flow through a series of sun salutations and on to warrior poses. I love warrior poses. I fashion myself a warrior calling on that inner spirit to face all manner of things in my life that scare me -- from picking out a birthday present for my boyfriend (what if he doesn't like it?) to*

showing up at my first creative writing class at FIU (what if they hate my writing?). I visualize this great warrior riding on a sensual and powerful galloping horse the color of caramel. He brandishes a large bow in his left hand. It is strong and taut, the arrows unbendable traveling a precise path to their target. I also fashion this great warrior within as a woman in iron-mesh armor, wielding a large silver sword studded with precious stones, specks of blood on the blade, an iron shield protecting her from assault.

These warriors help me survive the perils of this world and navigate the shark infested waters of my mind. They rest only when it's safe. They're only a breath away, on the yoga mat, yet I do not return to the mat for weeks on end. Why do I resist visiting the mat? What do I fear? The narrow path to liberation? Or is it liberation itself?

And so, the yoga mat, sticky and purple, sits idle in the trunk of my car, waiting to be called to action."

Clearly, I had already noticed one of the emotional and spiritual benefits of yoga – connecting me to an inner strength that I felt I needed in order to encounter what I perceived as the world's outer threats and the dangers of my undisciplined mind. I just hadn't found a teacher who could introduce me to the fullness of yoga and the gifts it offered, and who could guide me through the obstacles that prevented me from establishing a disciplined practice.

I needed to disavow myself of this idea that yoga was exercise, a wimpy one at that, and only something I would do sporadically to stretch my hamstrings in between runs. Cancer took care of that. Suddenly, my body was unable to run, or exercise with the vigor I thought was required to subjugate my thighs into an acceptable shape. I was forced into surrender by the fatigue caused by treatment until corpse pose, or *savasana*, became my pose of choice. Restorative yoga felt a little *too passive*, but it was also enjoyable and, in an unexpected way, revitalizing.

I was already practicing *vypassana,* or Buddhist insight meditation. I was a fan of Joseph Goldstein and Jack Kornfield, and had embraced this form of meditation because I could do it anywhere, at any time, throughout my day. All it required was that I became aware, in the present moment, of my breath, my body, and my thoughts, with curiosity and without judgment. Vypassana, in essence, means to see things as they are. It means being in reality, rather than in the stories in my head. My breath, my feet moving on the ground, my internal sensations, and the world around me, all can serve as anchors to bring me back to this one moment. Grounded in this one moment, the only moment there is, I can observe the stream of thoughts – the ticker tape of my mind – moving through without attaching meaning, or "buying into" the story, and gain insight into how my mind works (in its skillful and unskillful patterns alike). With *vypassana,* I started to become detached enough from my inner experience that emotions could arise and dissipate without getting stuck. *Vypassana* allowed me to go through my first chemotherapy session without much suffering at all, much to my surprise.

What I did not have, was a formal sitting practice. The rebel in me resisted the idea of discipline, of having to sit at a particular time of day, for a particular length of time. This "rebel without a clue" remains a close friend of mine, a shadow aspect of myself, the residue of my addictive nature. I needed a teacher. I could not continue to just learn from books and tapes, or CDs, or periodic workshops. I needed a teacher to whom I could submit for guidance.

But how does one find a teacher? My only teacher had been my own inner guru, who had sweetly and gently guided me to the next helpful stretch in my journey, placing in my path the resources I needed to continue on. I believe this inner guru led me to my embodied teacher because I was open, and ready, to be guided.

I always had a resistance to following a teacher or guru who required worship and adulation. I did not want a man in white robes and a long beard who set himself apart from the world as a special being, or a superstar who was visibly full of ego and a desire to be admired. I thought maybe it was my own ego and its resistance to submit to someone else's guidance.

Eventually, I realized it was wise discernment. A student must become worthy of the teacher, for sure. But a teacher has to demonstrate his worthiness to the students as well through the embodiment of the teachings. A true teacher lives the teachings, and they radiate the truth that they live. I wanted a teacher who would guide me to my own inner guiding light.

"Seek and you shall find, knock and it shall be opened unto you," Jesus said. I was seeking. Even below the level of my conscious awareness, I was "praying" through my desire to be guided into an even deeper spiritual understanding and experience.

"I want to grow by leaps and bounds in spiritual understanding" had been one of my most fervent affirmations. The idea had been opening me up to receive what I desired, even if it wasn't perfectly clear to me in what shape the manifestation would show up. But show up it did.

In 2008, I meet Chanti, a young Cuban-American woman with straight brown hair cascading down to her sacrum who teaches yoga at the eating disorder treatment center where I work as a psychotherapist. Chanti teaches the patients yoga philosophy and practices to gain insight into themselves, rather than just physical poses and breathing. I am intrigued by her approach.

I begin attending her classes at a yoga studio where the practice rooms have altars instead of mirrors. The classes start with instructions to center around an intention, focusing on the breath, working with energy, and gently increasing the challenge of the poses. After a peak of intensity, the class begins its slow descent toward seated poses and rest, or *savasana*. Classes always end with pranayama and a brief meditation.

This spiritually-focused practice is something I can embrace, so I begin to attend classes regularly, adding workshops to broaden my understanding and experience of deeper practices – *bandhas* or energy locks, *pranayama*, which is the science of breath, and *yamas* and *niyamas*, the ethical guidelines that must precede all practice.

The more I practice, the more I notice my tendencies. There are poses I avoid because they scare me. And there are poses I push too hard into, not heeding the principle of *ahimsa*, or non-harming. As I have with running, I continue to create stress in my body and to get injured.

But my main desire is to meditate on a regular basis. I want to have a discipline, and to stick with it. But I also *hate* to do anything, in any context – work, family, and even the spiritual life -- that feels like an obligation, a *should*, or a *must*. This is my main obstacle. I can't seem to find the balance between effort and surrender, between *sukha* (ease) and *sthira* (steadiness). My life continues to be a study in extremes: behaviors, thoughts and feelings swinging like a pendulum from one edge to the other with no balance or middle path.

Admittedly, my desire to meditate on a regular basis is tinged with an ego-driven need to "achieve more spirituality." On the other hand, it is also my Soul's desire to know the bliss of its nature. Both are true.

Chanti embodies a sense of ease in perfect harmony with a visible confidence that is not conceited or boastful. Her interactions with the class are benevolent and invite the student to embrace self-compassion instead of increase competitiveness or the drive to "achieve a perfect pose." She teaches us mantras, Sanskrit words infused with sound vibrations that hold powers or *shaktis*. We chant these mantras before class, or after class, sometimes during class depending on the goal. Chanti's humility, acceptance and grace makes me willing to ask her to teach me, and I begin to engage in private sessions with her.

"I want to learn to do headstand," I say when she asks what my goals are.

"Why?" she asks.

"Because I want to conquer the fear that stops me from doing it," I reply. Fear has manifested in my life in many forms. Fear has blocked me from fulfilling many of my life's desires. I want to conquer fear in all its forms.

I tell her that I also want to deepen my spirituality, and to heal from all the ravages that cancer treatment and over-exercise have laid waste on my body.

"We can work with that," she says, and I trust her.

Our sessions are held in a small room that only holds a small altar, mats and yoga props like bolsters, straps and blocks. She walks me through the poses with mindfulness, helping me to slowly build up my strength and my capacity, attending to the emotional impediments with gentleness and non-judgment.

I learn to stand on my head by strengthening my core and floating up from that center. I learn to conquer the fear of the pose when doing it against the wall, but not in the middle of the room. I eventually stop standing on my head to avoid further injury to my cervical spine, and because I understand now that what yoga has to offer is so much more than an ability to master physical poses. I begin to understand that harnessing energy, or *prana*, and accessing deeper states of meditation are much more important and quite doable without excessive *asana*. I learn to do "smart" *asana* – asana practices intelligently sequenced to create a specific energetic quality to support my meditation practice.

Through self-study and self-understanding, my goal changed from wanting to overcome the fear of standing on my head, to mastering my resistance to sit. Chanti instructed me to harness *prana* through the practice of *prana dharana*, a tantric practice that uses awareness and breath to concentrate the universal life energy at the eye center.

I had first learned *prana dharana* from Pandit Rajmani Tigunait, lovingly known as Panditji to his students, during a Living Tantra weekend workshop he conducted in Miami. Panditji is the spiritual head of the Himalayan Institute and successor to Swami Rama of the Himalayas, founder of the institute in the United States. Panditji is a master, initiated by Swami Rama in the five-thousand-year-old tradition of the Himalayan masters back in 1976. He holds two doctoral degrees in Sanskrit and Oriental Studies and has been teaching and lecturing internationally for decades.

Despite the impressive curriculum, he impressed me most with his humility. I observed that he was not trying to look like a guru. He wore plain slacks and a short-sleeved, button-down shirt. He was friendly and accessible and not stand-offish. He appeared to treat others as equals rather than as subservient or less-than. He was not pulling for admiration or adulation.

"This is a guru I can learn from," I thought to myself, as I delighted in understanding Tantra for what it is, not for what it is thought to be. Tantra is not about sexual pleasure, as it is mistakenly understood in the West. Nor is it about magical practices, as it is known to be in the East. Tantra is an ancient spiritual science whose practices are designed to help us optimize our life on this earthly plane of existence, to be successful both spiritually and in the world. Through hatha yoga, pranayama, mantras, yantras, kriyas, mudras, and rituals, we can achieve a life of both worldly and spiritual prosperity. It is, indeed, about the "marriage" of humanity and divinity, of Shiva and Shakti.

These were principles that had been informing my life for years. I just didn't have a name for it. I had even presented a workshop on the marriage of humanity and divinity at Unity on the Bay, my spiritual home in Miami. I had been gently but persistently guided by an internal wisdom away from dissociative spirituality to embodied spirituality. Tantra provided a framework, one proven by thousands of year of tradition. I was home.

Chanti reminded me to use the practice of *prana dharana* to begin my meditation, and assigned me a mantra to do *mantra japa*, or the mental repetition of the mantra to awaken its energy vibrations and power.

"How many repetitions should I do?" I asked, already focused on a goal, an "achievement" that, if not met, would reinforce my sense of failure and inadequacy, my ingrained pattern of feeling like I'm not doing enough, and I'm not good enough.

"As soon as you no longer sense *prana*," she instructed, "you stop the practice."

"Oh," this was a new idea for me. "Are you sure?"

"If you do only one round of the *malas*, but you do it with *prana*, that will be more meaningful than if you make yourself do one thousand repetitions without *prana*," she admonished. I remembered Saint Teresa of Avila's admonition to her nuns to practice praying the rosary with devotion, rather than like parrots.

Of course, we had already established that anything I felt obligated to do, I would resist and not want to do. So the idea of only doing practices when the energy was present made sense. I began to do one round of japa, or 108 repetitions, and soon, because the energy was there, and I was drawn by the energy to continue, I began to do two rounds, or 216 repetitions.

The mantra that I was assigned to repeat was the Maha Mrityunjaya, a healing mantra representing the power to conquer illness, pain and suffering as well as the fear of death. In addition, this mantra is believed to increase courage and determination. It was perfect.

Rolf Sovick, president and spiritual director at the Himalayan Institute, writes in an article about the Mrityunjaya Mantra that Lord Shiva himself gave humanity this mantra to overcome the fear of death. The mantra, he writes, restores health, happiness and vitality. It also is helpful, in his view, for those working in the healing profession, for it draws the radiant Shakti of this mantra to prevent burnout.

I needed this mantra for many reasons: the years of self-abuse combined with chemotherapy, radiation and hormone suppression treatments had left me riddled with body pain–disc herniation in the cervical, thoracic and lumbar spines; inflammation and imbalance in the joints of the hips that caused me intense pain in the left hip and knee; torn ligaments in the right shoulder; and a chronic pattern of tension and pain in neck and shoulders. You name it, it hurt. And I was tired. My body was exhausted, fatigued and depleted. My mind was active, but my body lethargic.

I also needed courage, and lots of it, in order to move into the life my soul wanted to create, to move away from traditional paradigms into the non-traditional, to conquer the fear of death from cancer, yes, but also the fear of judgment and rejection.

Because I was using this mantra to heal the body and instill courage and perseverance, I was asked to concentrate the mind at the navel center. Manipura chakra, located at the navel, is said to be the center of will and determination, the fire center in the body that contains and distributes the life force. Contemplating this chakra, therefore, can help conquer disease.

As part of my "treatment" I was to surrender to the fact that I could not engage in strenuous exercise during this period of time, and was to do only very gentle and restorative poses guided by the breath. I was to let the breath lead the movements. I did less and less asana, no running at all, and very little if any aerobic exercise, only nurturing movements that would not strain my body.

Gradually, I began to experience less pain, and more vitality. I was able to conquer the fear of following my soul's calling. I started to fall in love with the Maha Mrityunjaya, a mantra that I did not find appealing at first. I loved the Gayatri Mantra. I wanted to do the Gayatri Mantra. But as my teachers have taught me, what I want is not always what I need.

My practice led me to apply to study with Yogarupa Rod Stryker, Chanti's teacher and a disciple of Pandit Rajmani Tinguait. I was called to apply for a ParaYoga Master Training. I followed the calling simply because it was there, as a way to deepen my understanding and practice of this Tantric lineage that felt like coming home.

The first workshop was held in Miami, which is one of the main reasons I applied to attend. It was called *Vinyasa Krama*, or the "wise progression"

of poses and breathing to extract their maximum benefit. I was concerned about this workshop because I imagined it would contain intense asana practice, and I had been doing almost no physical practice. My ego was worried, "how will I be able to keep up? People will think I'm a wimp."

"Don't worry," Chanti said. "Just listen to your body and stop when you need to. Let the assistants know that you have limitations."

The workshop did require a lot of demanding physical practices, every morning and every afternoon. But, true to the workshop's name, and the gift and experience of the teacher, the practices were intelligently sequenced to keep them safe even for me. My ego did get in the way, and from time to time the assistants had to whisper in my ear, "You may want to hold back a little," which was helpful since my own wise mind, or *buddhi*, was not yet fully online when it came to holding back from excess.

What amazed me was that I was able to do a lot more than I thought I could do because the class was infused with *prana*. *Prana* was leading the movements. And the meditations were so deep that I felt as if I'd touched the proverbial kingdom of heaven. My spine was filled with *prana*, ergo I *was* a yogi.

Walking back to the MetroRail to return home after one particularly delightful meditation experience, I was filled with such an intense bliss that I could not contain it. In Matthew 13:44-46, Jesus speaks of a merchant who has found a pearl of great price, and having found it, went and sold all he had and bought it.

"This is the pearl of great price!" I thought. "I am willing to *'sell all I have'* to pursue this path." I became a devoted ParaYoga student in that moment, and chose to surrender to my new teacher, whom I know as Yogarupa.

To "sell all I have" meant that I would let go of old ideas and embrace new ones. It meant that I would invest of my time and treasure into learning and practicing this new wisdom. It meant that I would pursue more training and even initiation. I was so willing to go to any length that I signed up for a training in February in Minnesota because it would allow me to take a more advanced training in Colorado the next spring. It meant reading more books by Pandit Rajmani Tinguait and Swami Rama, in one of which I recognized the face of the guru that appeared to me during my *samadhi* experience at age thirteen in Nicaragua – it was Swami Rama! Swami Rama as a younger man, when he was known as Bhole Baba.

Could it be? I wondered. Could it be that I was destined to belong to this lineage? Was this the guru I had been waiting for all those years? I keep going back to the image of Bhole Baba, Swami Rama as a young man, on the green leaf of the tree in my backyard in Las Colinas, in 1974 when I was only thirteen, an image I assumed came from the collective unconscious or some previously recorded idea of what a Hindu guru must look like. It still may be the case, but when I saw the picture of Swami Rama as Bhole Baba in the book by Panditji, *At the Eleventh Hour*, it was so familiar that I cried. I cried tears of joy in the recognition and marvel at the serendipitous nature of the journey of life.

Healing is not without doubt. Mind resists healing. Yogarupa says that these are *samskaras*, or imprints left in the subconscious mind from life experiences. But *prana* can dissolve these *samskaras*, which is why the daily and consistent practice of yoga in all its dimensions can transform our lives and eliminate the effects of negative karma.

The daily recitation of mantras imbued with healing power can transform our minds and even our bodies at a structural level. I really believe this, and have experienced it, and yet, I doubt. How human of me!

One particular morning, after about three weeks of leading into my meditation practice with a healing kriya, I feel the entire right side of my upper body – my right torso, right shoulder, right arm, and wrist recently injured again with De Quervain's tendonitis – begin to soften, open, fill with prana, and experience complete freedom from pain. And what does my mind do? Go into a complete panic.

I am sitting there in a half-lotus position, eyes closed, anchored in the observer, and this is what I notice: My hand continuing to thumb through the mala beads, the subtle energy infusing the right side of my body, the resonance of my *guru mantra*, and on the surface of the mind a rapid-fire sequence of thoughts.

Thoughts like ripples on a lake, disturbing the surface, and screaming, "But (but, but, but) isn't aging, illness, pain and death inherent in our human existence? If I believe in the power of awareness to heal me, won't I suffer if or when I become ill again and die? Shouldn't I accept illness, pain and death as a way to stop suffering about them? If I trust that I am healed, won't I be more shocked if (or when) I receive a diagnosis, or feel pain again? (A form of pre-traumatic stress disorder?).

Thankfully, a witness still online, I was able to return to just observing breath, energy and mantra, and a more calming voice stating "Your will not mine be done; if it is your will that I shall be healed, let it be so." Didn't Jesus say to those he cured, "Believe, and you shall be healed"? Why shouldn't I believe, then?

Ten years of remission, cancer free, health restored, I choose to believe that I am healed. Not to mention, twenty-seven years in remission from alcoholism and drug addiction; almost two decades in remission from suicidal depression, bulimia and anorexia; a life-long journey of transformation from self-hatred and self-destruction to self-love and a love of the embodied life. Why shouldn't I believe, then?

Reflections

Our beliefs infuse our values. It therefore behooves us to understand what it is that we believe, consciously or unconsciously, because it these beliefs – even hidden ones – that are shaping our lives, that which we think, feel and do.

In his book *The Biology of Belief: Unleashing the Power of Consciousness, Matter, & Miracles,* Dr. Bruce Lipton challenges the existing scientific paradigm that our genes determine our life by illuminating the interconnection between the energy of our beliefs, our lifestyle practices and the subsequent behavior of our cells. The growing science of epigenetics is now clearly outlining that genes don't necessarily express unless triggered by environment, including the environment of stress created by our negative patterns of thinking.

As you believe, so it is. "Go. As you have believed, let it be done for you" Jesus said to the centurion seeking healing for another (Matthew 8:13). "Everything is possible for one who believes," he said elsewhere, and referred to the power to move mountains with belief as small as a mustard seed. Christian or not, I want to pay attention to this teaching.

If I believe eating fruits and vegetables will help my health and make me feel better, I will eat fruits and vegetables. If I don't, I won't do it. If I believe meditation will improve my life, I will do it and experience its rewards. If not, I might do it half-heartedly with no good effect.

Modern science has established that sometimes we heal because of a "placebo" effect. But what of "nocebo"? It follows that if we believe something won't work, it won't. Or if we believe it will have an adverse effect, then it will. Our minds are very powerful, and we want to investigate the beliefs we are holding, consciously and unconsciously, that are shaping our lives. And it's not just a matter of simple affirmations. You can affirm until the cows come home, but if deep inside you hold an opposite belief, your perception of life will continue to present you with information validating that deeply ingrained thought pattern.

The Vedas call this *vikalpa,* a deep-driving desire that was perhaps formed by traumatic experiences and takes you away from your highest values and authentic, intrinsic potential. Addictions and eating disorders would fall under the category of *vikalpa*-driven behaviors. In his book *The Four Desires: Creating a Life of Purpose, Happiness, Prosperity, and*

Freedom, Rod Stryker provides a methodology for uncovering both a life's purpose and the means to achieve it, as well as the obstacles and how to conquer them.

Acceptance and Commitment Therapy (ACT), also proposes that in order to conquer depression, anxiety, and problem behaviors, one must lead a values-driven life. When the values you have set for yourself are more powerful than the mood-driven behaviors, change is possible.

Dr. Stephen Hayes, who developed ACT, in essence stated that you can act on values regardless of the emotions you experience by accepting your emotions and defusing charged cognitions. ACT has been studied in populations with eating disorders and found to be effective. It is not uncommon to find ACT as one of the modalities used in residential treatment centers.

The centerpiece of ACT is to identify values, or supreme concerns. Values are defined as principles or standards of behavior, or one's judgment of what is important in life. When you know what's important to you, then you can go about establishing a roadmap to reach that destination. If you value honesty, for example, you can decide how to bring that value concretely into your daily life. You will take steps to be honest even when it causes you anxiety and you want to avoid it. You can accept that you are uncomfortable being honest, stay present, and choose to take an action that honors your value despite the barriers.

To create a values-driven life we must begin by identifying beliefs and assessing if we still hold them to be true once we understand their source (e.g. they were our parents' beliefs but not necessarily our own). Next, we clarify the values that are important to us. And finally, we can create a roadmap that will take us to that destination we want to reach. Once focused on our values, we will be less influenced by emotion-driven self-destructive behaviors. Other things become more important than the drive for thinness, looking a certain way, or fitting into a particular pair of jeans.

Journaling Exercises

1. Values are what we find meaningful in life. They are what we care about and consider important. Some examples of values are: family, career, success, happiness, integrity, honesty, health, connection, community, contribution, creativity, education, and spirituality. Write a list of your most cherished values.

   ____
   ____
   ____
   ____
   ____

2. List ways in which you can bring your values into your life in concrete ways. For example, health. If health is important, how can you resolve to take care of your body?

   ____
   ____
   ____
   ____
   ____

3. Journal: If you were able to live your value, how would that change your life?

   ____
   ____
   ____
   ____
   ____

4. Write: If you were unable to live your value, how will that impact your life?

   ____
   ____
   ____
   ____
   ____

5. Identify the obstacles to living your value. Consider what thoughts, feelings, sensations or urges arise as you feel yourself moving toward your valued life.

   ____

   ____

   ____

   ____

   ____

6. What gets in the way of you acting on your value? Are values clashing? For example, you want a healthy body, but you also want to self-soothe using food. How can you resolve that dialectical conflict?

   ____

   ____

   ____

   ____

   ____

7. What are your thoughts on the term "spiritual bypassing"? Do you use spiritual strategies to avoid feeling distress? How does spirituality help or hinder your recovery?

   ____

   ____

   ____

   ____

   ____

8. What if you could acknowledge the difficulty in your life without seeking to avoid it? Could you observe the feelings and sensations instead of pushing them away?

   ____

   ____

   ____

   ____

   ____

9. Meditation is a form of self-study. When you meditate you come face to face with both your light and your shadow, your virtues and your faults. Do you meditate? Why? Why not? What happens when you meet your light? What happens when you meet your shadow?

   ____

   ____

   ____

   ____

   ____

10. Ultimately, the goal is to transform and transcend, but we can't transform or transcend what remains hidden. What other forms of self-study and self-examination do you use? How rigorous are you in self-examination?

    ____

    ____

    ____

    ____

    ____

CHAPTER 12

Express Your Self: Transforming Symptoms into Authenticity

I am going to tell you about Sri Vidya. I feel my heart flutter and leap. We are sitting on our yoga mats in a large open room flanked by floor-to-ceiling windows facing the frozen tundra outside. The snow is several feet high on the golf course. It has been nineteen below zero for three nights in a row and the temperature has not risen above freezing since I arrived in Minneapolis for this yoga training with Yogarupa, a man I now call my teacher. I am fifty-two years old and a long way from Managua, where I was born to my icy but stable German father and a mother as volatile as the land on which we lived. Fertile with creativity yet fiercely destructive, her silence was as cutting as her words and her five-foot stature projected a seven-foot shadow that trapped me in a suffocating grip.

At the time of my birth, Nicaragua was a country about to be ripped in half by a bloody civil war, its lakes not powerful enough to cool the fires of a string of volcanos that make the earth rumble and tremble, or the political fires of a people tired of decades of dictatorship. I was born in 1961, at the dawn of a new era of rebellion and discord. It was the year the *Frente Sandinista de Liberación Nacional* came into existence, and a group of idealists began to plot the bloody overthrow of a decades-long dictatorship in the country of my birth. The Nicaraguan civil war raged as I entered into adolescence, an outward extension of the war within my family and my endless battle for the right to take up space, to breathe my own air, to exist without having to compromise my authenticity to fit a mold and be accepted. War, external and internal, ripped apart everything that held me together in one piece.

My attempts at creating order out of the chaos of my youth gave way to a rigid perfectionism that left no room for error. I longed for a sense of permanence, solidity, and identity, for some semblance of meaning and belonging in the midst of the personal, social, cultural and political upheaval that framed my upbringing – and I accomplished this by staying tight and small to contain any exuberance that might call attention or invite rejection.

The Russian missile crisis, the Bay of Pigs invasion, JFK's and Martin Luther King's assassinations, the Vietnam War, protest marches and the anti-war movement, the sexual revolution, the birth of feminism, the civil rights movement, transcendental meditation, LSD and psilocybin psychedelic explorations into altered states of consciousness, peace, love, Rock & Roll and flights to the moon. This was the backdrop of my formative years. Despite that, even my attempts at rebellion were controlled and measured. I used drugs to escape, not to expand my consciousness beyond its limited confines.

Yogarupa continues to speak, and not without hesitation. *Perhaps I shouldn't be speaking about this.* He laughs, vacillating because the audio system has cut out three times since he began his talk. Sri Vidya being an ancient Tantric lineage from the Himalayas, a wisdom that was hidden for eons, he pauses to asses if the audio difficulties are a message to maintain its secrets.

My heart takes another leap and silently cries out, *please don't stop!* My yearning to know and experience this wisdom feels urgent. It is a wisdom that views the creative impulse that generated the very universe we inhabit as a feminine force, a Divine Mother, and the human body as Her abode, when for most of my life I viewed my body only as a source of suffering, a fleshly prison of tissues and bone to be escaped from through any means available – alcohol, drugs, food, sex, suicide, and yes, even transcendental meditation and all forms of disembodied spirituality.

Sri Vidya literally means auspicious wisdom, or supreme knowledge, the knowledge of the Self, and its goal is to lead us to a direct experience of ourselves as "a wave of beauty and bliss arising from the ocean of pure consciousness." Sri Vidya is devoted to the Divine Mother, the divine feminine principle which is seen as the cause of all creation. She is pure consciousness. She is the absolute, non-dual, ultimate reality in which the appearing dual manifestation of Shiva, the masculine force of pure undifferentiated consciousness, and Shakti, the manifesting or feminine force of creation, only appear to dance as separate but are always one and the same.

As he continues to teach the elemental aspects of this oral tradition, whose transmission from teacher to student has been unbroken for many thousands of years, that which moved within my heart bursts as a dam that is cracked and floods every arid inch of land around it.

My tears flow without restraint, tears that speak to the endless gratitude I feel to be alive in this moment and to have survived my strange compulsion to die.

I am here! My soul exclaims. *I am alive!*

A continuous string of memories flows with the flood, like black pearls knotted together with soft string: the early years of insomnia and night terrors, the later years of self-destructive alcohol and drug abuse, the starvation and bulimia that decimated my body, the first time I wanted to kill myself at fifteen after my parents discovered I'd had sex with a twenty-one-year-old man after his sister's wedding, the last time I planned a suicide at age thirty because my bipolar boyfriend could not decide whether he wanted to marry me or leave me, the abusive marriage that I narrowly escaped with my life, a cancer diagnosis and months of grueling chemotherapy, and the time my mother threatened to cut me into sixty-four pieces, which might explain the subtle lines that scar my forearms, reminders of my self-loathing.

Concurrently, as diamonds illuminating the darkness of these black pearls of experience, I witness memories of the time I experienced oneness with all of life at the age of thirteen after meditating on a mantra for thirty minutes, the prayer groups and bible studies I sought out to find solace from my suffering, the Native-American sweat lodges and Kirtan chanting and crystal bowl meditations that I pursued through the years in an attempt to overcome my own self-hatred, the bolt of lightning that shot through me the day I begged to be relieved of the compulsion to drink, the warmth that flooded me when I asked the universe to comfort me after a miscarriage.

Flashes of images begin to weave together the fragments of my life into a cohesive whole, like a patchwork quilt whose individual pieces of fabric become a tapestry filled with meaning.

As the snow continues to fall outside, the tears stream down my face, along the sides of my neck, through my collar bones, and in between my breasts. I feel the familiar tickle of shame threatening to erupt in my belly, and notice the thoughts of worry that I might be perceived as emotionally unstable. I notice shame's attempt to coil itself around my esophagus like a poisonous snake, but refuse to stifle the flow because they are tears of gratitude, of love for this Divine Mother whose hand has been guiding me step by step through each tragic incident to this moment.

The irony that somehow, through no design of my own, I have landed in a spiritual tradition that worships the feminine divine is not lost on me, whose mother's womb felt inhospitable before I could take my first breath. From the moment I was conceived, her nicotine-laced womb, the only universe I knew, repelled me. I know that it will be difficult to many of you to believe that memories of our experiences in the womb are accessible when we explore implicitly encoded memories somatically. I believe that I did not want to incarnate. At least that is the sense I had during many bodywork sessions where I connected to my intrauterine experiences. I know that I spent half my life trying to escape the places I felt I did not belong –my country, my family, my very own body.

I am here! My soul sings again, recognizing the winding road to returning, or arriving for the first time, to a sense of belonging. *I am alive!* I take a look outside as the trickle of tears slows, then stops. The white expanse calms me. Having waged the war between my impulse to live and my longing to die, I have passionately embraced an existence I once condemned, and a body I once despised. On this frigid winter day, I am a long way from the land in which I was born, and yet, I am home. I survived a cunning compulsion to self-destruct just long enough to comfortably take up residence in my skin, in this life, in this world.

ꝺ

I always had an affinity for the feminine divine, maybe because, despite my mother's best efforts, I rarely felt mothered. Or maybe because I could not accept that God had a gender, and it was male. In college, I read the then newly-published book *When God Was a Woman* by Merlin Stone, who gave resounding archeological evidence that women's roles were radically different when cultures worshipped the Goddess, before religion was overtaken by a patriarchal socio-cultural structure and the women were degraded to the point of blaming Eve for the "fall of man." I wanted to worship a Goddess, but felt that my only options were Wicca or paganism, which I had no interest in pursuing. I clung to the sentence in Genesis 1:27 that states that "God created human beings in its own image. In the image of God it created them; male and female he created them." Therefore, my logic reasoned, God is either both male and female, or God is *neither* male *nor* female.

In the depths of a dark depression, and in the grips of the persistently severe torture of an eating disorder, I remember calling on the Mother – in those days Mary, mother of Jesus. I was in an outpatient program for my eating disorder, a few short weeks out from a too-short and inadequate two-week in-patient stay. The program was near Hialeah, a long and painful drive in rush-hour traffic on the Palmetto Expressway (more like a parking lot) from my home in Kendall. I refused to gain weight, and the program was threatening to hospitalize me against my will and force-feed me through a nasogastric tube.

"We only want you to get to one hundred pounds!" they would say in an exasperated tone.

"But I'm only five-feet tall!" was my retort of choice. "Ninety-two pounds is enough!"

The groups were held at night. I was tired and depressed. It was unbearable to be asked to identify and label my emotions, and to share them openly with a group of strangers. Looking back, I cannot remember a single face in that group. The only thing I remember is the story of one individual whose self-harm behavior was picking at her skin, popping the blackheads on her face until she bled, or pinching her arms with her fingernails until she broke the skin. I can't remember her face or her name, but I remember the story. I could relate to her expressions of self-hatred. Other than that, I did not feel connected to anyone or anything. So on one of those nights, when the pain was so unbearable that I cried and screamed in the car on the dark highway all the way to Kendall, I decided to drive even further south to St. Louis Catholic church, which had a prayer chapel open round-the-clock. I sat in front of the statue of Mary, my arms wrapped around my bony body, rocking and sobbing until I felt her spiritual embrace. Once I felt rocked to her spiritual bosom, I calmed down, I made it home, I did not binge or purge, and I did not kill myself. Ergo, I must need mothering, and since there were no human mothers to do it, I would pursue the comfort of the feminine divine.

When I got to Unity on the Bay in 2001, it took me a while to be able to pray to the "Father, Mother God." To retrain myself, I started to say the Our Father as Our Mother. I modified the prayer even further by removing the reference to "evil" with "ego" since I felt that the only temptation away from goodness was created by a fear-ridden and greedy ego, an ego afraid of losing something it has or not getting something it craves. I was not ready yet to worship the "mother," but I was convinced that God was not only a "father." I still did not understand what it meant for God to have both feminine and masculine aspects; until I began to pursue with diligence the study of yoga, in particular the comprehensive science of Tantric yoga, with a focus on Sri Vidya.

Sri Vidya is one of the ten Mahavidyas, or supreme paths to ultimate realization. Sri Vidya literally means auspicious wisdom, or supreme knowledge, and its goal – according to the Living Tantra program taught by the Himalayan Institute—is to lead us to "a direct experience of ourselves as a wave of beauty and bliss arising from the ocean of pure consciousness."

As I read, or hear, commentary on sacred texts describing these elusive, powerful, divine ideas, I am comforted. Finally, there is an explanation to the questions that plagued me since that day in kindergarten when I wondered why it was so bad that Eve wanted to have the knowledge of good and evil, since I questioned why God was only known as Father while Mother took a subservient role, since I made my first attempts to understand the story of Genesis when God created us "male and female" in God's own image. More importantly, I was comforted because I could experience myself as wave of bliss and delight, instead of experiencing my humanity as a "vale of tears," and my body as a prison to be escaped.

In *The Transformative Power of the Goddesses of Yoga*, Sally Kempton, a writer, teacher, and contemplative Tantrika, tells us that "the divine feminine has a thousand names and a thousand moods, but when she chooses to show up for you, she very often shows up as ecstasy." She also reminds us that "without her presence, Shiva cannot act in the world."

Shakti is the innate power in reality to be conscious, to know, and to create, and in the Tantric tradition, all of reality is her expression. She nudges us to evolve our consciousness. She is our hope to create a new reality.

In the Christian book of Revelation, "a new heaven and a new earth" come into existence and are described as "a bride beautifully dressed." She is "God's dwelling place," She is us, we are Her. And, the book tells us, when this happens, "there will be no more death or mourning or crying or pain, for the old order of things has passed away."

Because Tantra is basically a set of teachings and practices to help us embody this divine Shakti, it is essentially a Goddess path, according to Kempton. She describes the creative surge of Shakti and how the Tantrics view Shakti as having disguised herself by "disappearing into the tapestry" of creation. This MahaShakti is the force of life in all things, the power behind the breath, She Who Supports the World.

❧

Sally sat quietly in the front of the room, face with no make-up yet radiant with infused light, waiting for us to settle on our yoga mats and zafus at the Solstice Center in Boulder, Colorado. Some forty of us, mostly women plus a scattering of men, young and old, were to spend the next three hours practicing to "awaken Shakti" in her various aspects. She begins with a guided meditation and recitation of *bija,* or seed, mantras to invite the goddess to our midst.

We chant to Kali, and to Durga, and to Saraswati, three of the most commonly recognized version of Shakti. We meditate on Kali as the destroyer of ignorance, on Durga the protector riding on her lion, and Saraswati, goddess of creativity and insight. After each meditation, Sally answered questions and told stories about the metaphors of the goddess myths.

I want to find an affinity with one of these goddesses, with the qualities they express, or what they symbolize. Maybe Saraswati, to imbue me with creativity, or Lalita Tripura Sundari, the goddess of embodied spiritual bliss. But I identify most with Chinnamasta, the headless one. Her image is terrifying. She holds a cleaver in one hand, and her cut-off head in the other. Three streams of blood flow from her severed neck, one flowing into her severed head and the other two to her attendants. Not at all an image I want to identify myself with.

And yet, Chinnamasta represents "the radical transformation of the ego." She cuts off her own head, the ego, in the interest of truth, transmuting the pain and passions of life so they become a fountain of nourishment and bliss for the practitioner and her disciples. Out of the darkness flows life energy and wisdom. Chinnamasta is recognized in egoless states and "naked truthfulness no matter what the cost," writes Sally. In the shadow side, a Jungian analyst quoted in the book has associated her with bulimics. Those who want to "die before you die" will invoke Chinnamasta for help, and she must have been with me as I conquered the fear of death while undergoing cancer treatment. She is also to be invoked for help with deep surrender into meditative states. She is the "thunderbolt lightning of spiritual awakening." I am pleased to have discovered Chinnamasta, an aspect of the goddess I did not previously know, consciously, but was engaged in a relationship with in my life as the drive to dissolve ego, to be in truth, and to grow spiritually "by leaps and bounds."

"The human is the hallowed. If you hallow this life you meet the living God."
Martin Buber, I and Thou

After my cancer diagnosis, I thought I would die at fifty-one. It was just a strong presentiment, the number fifty-one loudly flashing in my mind's eye. Also, my good friend Patty had died exactly eight years after her diagnosis with a similar strand of breast cancer, and she'd been born only one month before I was.

Here is what I would have wanted people to say about me at my funeral if I had:

> "She became transparent to the world."
> "She was not afraid to stand up for what she believed."
> "She had the courage to speak the truth with love and compassion."
> "She made a choice to honor her needs and heal completely."
> "She was strong, and curious, and shared her gifts freely."
> "She was at ease in her body and open to love."
> "She embodied what she taught."
> "She was unstoppable in her quest to embody the Divine."
> "She rejoiced and delighted in living, traveling, connecting and creating."

But the truth was that I had not yet mustered the courage to live authentically, boldly and courageously. I still sought to protect myself from discomfort, especially the fear of displeasing others or ruffling feathers. I wanted to avoid judgment and criticism above all, even if it meant neglecting my needs and denying my desires. I felt terror if others disapproved. I wanted to be loved even if it meant giving up my authentic self, which is a contradiction in itself because such love would never feel genuine. I longed to be fully myself but it felt like an impossible task.

I had more work to do, if I was to live as I was meant to, with purpose.

The decade since my cancer diagnosis was one of the most fruitful in my evolution – personally, professionally, psychologically and spiritually.

Indeed, I have made it to fifty-four, thus far committed to living a life of complete authenticity and transparency. This book is a manifestation of that commitment. When the shame of being rejected or the terror of being ridiculed arises, I say "bring it on! I can take it!" Shame no longer has a binding and immobilizing effect, neither does it make me sick to my stomach. It has become nothing but a smoke monster, quickly dissipating with each breath I take.

I choose life, with all of its hues and nuances, the full spectrum of experience and emotion. This is the joy of living – being able to experience it all with equanimity.

Reflections

The choices I have made – sometimes consciously, sometimes unwittingly – have helped me to embrace life as an embodied being and to stop believing death was the only means to discard the sheath that obscured my soul and reclaim my divine nature. One could say that in the words of Martin Buber, I "hallowed this life" instead of continuing to live in the delusion that life in this world created a separation between me and Spirit, ripping my soul from its divine connection as if flesh and bone were a prison that removed me from my blissful nature of the divine.

Instead, what I have discovered through spiritual exploration and truth-seeking, is that my soul incarnated to overcome this delusion of separation, to understand that it is only the ego - *asmita* - the created one, who believes it is sole creator and ruler of reality, who believes it is only this flesh and this superficial mind. Soul is never separate from God. *Ayam ātmā brahma; aham brahmāsmi.* Atman is Brahman; I am as eternal as Brahman. That is our nature.

At three, I delighted in foraging for wild strawberries in Omama's garden. In my fifties, I delight in foraging for wild raspberries in the Colorado Rocky Mountains that are my new home. I've stopped warring with my body's hungers, and I honor my body as a temple of my soul. I do not compromise the health of my body, or the integrity of my soul, to weigh a certain number, or to wear a particular size of clothing. I dedicate myself to serving God in humanity by using my experience to help those who want to, as desperately as I did, to liberate themselves from the chains of their self-imposed and socially-reinforced (as eating disorders are) prisons.

My entire life's journey--walking through the valley of the shadow of death, the fear and terror of traumatic experiences, the descent into the pit of addictions and self-destruction, the difficult ascent back to the light--all of it has been purposeful and meaningful, *all of it* has contributed to my ability to sit with and embrace others with compassion and to support their healing.

Even those who seemingly do not want to heal, or are stuck in the self-created suffering of a darkened mind, are deserving of compassion. They are in the grips of an obfuscation, or *avidya*, so great that only a bright flash of illumination might awaken them from the slumber. I was once an actor in a melodrama written, produced, directed by me, and yet I did not know it. I had no idea that it had nothing to do with objective reality.

I believe in the potential for complete healing. I believe we can all be restored to the wholeness we were designed to express. Humanly divine and divinely human; we have the same qualities and powers, or *shaktis*, as gods, goddesses and timeless masters. This is a great responsibility.

"You must light your own lamp," the Buddha said. This means, we must practice. We must practice self-inquiry, renunciation of the ego's long-held erroneous beliefs, prayer, and deep meditation. If we are graced, we might awaken to our true, authentic nature.

"I assure you, he who believes in me, the works that I do he shall do also, and greater works than these shall he do." Jesus said. But we do not believe him, so we do not demonstrate our greatest potential. We remain small, fearful, constricted, and separate, judging and hating one another because we do not see our differences as beautiful expressions of divinity.

Who are you? What are you willing to believe? Will you practice and seek the truth, with a capital T, of an ultimate reality greater than your fear-based ego's limited perceptions? Will you unleash the energy bound in your symptoms and express your authentic self?

Journaling Exercises

1. Authenticity means the quality of being authentic and genuine, not false or copied. What does it meant to you to be genuine?

2. How do you imagine feeling if you were to be genuine?

3. How would you move if you moved authentically?

4. In what ways do you stifle your authenticity and become a false version of yourself?

5. Who do you copy and why?

6. How do you feel when you know you are wearing a mask and pretending to be someone you are not?

____

____

____

____

____

7. What's the worst that could happen if you were to be yourself?

____

____

____

____

____

8. What's the best that could happen?

____

____

____

____

____

9. If you were to unleash the power bound in your eating disorder symptoms, how much power would be available to you?

____

____

____

____

____

10. What is your relationship to that power? Do you fear it or trust it?

____

____

____

____

____

THE END

References

Introduction

Ainley, V. & Tsakiris, M. (2013). Body conscious? Interoceptive awareness measured by heartbeat perception is negatively correlated with self-objectification. *PLoS ONE, 8*(2), e55568.

Craig, A.D. (2014). *How do you Feel? An Interoceptive Moment with your Biological Self.* Princeton, NJ: Princeton University Press.

Damasio, A. (1994). *Descartes' Error: Emotion, Reason and the Human Brain.* New York, NY: Penguin Group.

Masters, R.A. (2010). *Spiritual Bypassing: When Spirituality Disconnects Us From What Really Matters.* Berkeley, CA: North Atlantic Books.

Schore, A.N. (1999). *Affect Regulation and the Origin of the Self: The Neurobiology of Emotional Development.* Hillsdale, NJ: Lawrence Erlbaum Associates.

Schore, A.N. (2003). *Affect Dysregulation and Disorders of the Self.* New York, NY: W.W. Norton.

Chapter 1

Briere, J. & Scott, C. (2007). Assessing of trauma symptoms in eating disordered populations. *Eating Disorders,* (15)347–358.

Chassler, L. (1997). Understanding anorexia nervosa and bulimia nervosa from an attachment perspective. *Clinical Social Work Journal, 25*(4), 407-423.

Damasio, A. (2000). *The Feeling of What Happens: Body and Emotion in the Making of Consciousness.* New York, NY: Mariner Books.

Everill, J., Waller, G., & Macdonald, W. (1995). Reported sexual abuse and bulimic symptoms: The mediating role of dissociation. *Dissociation, 8,* 155-159.

Lockwood, R., Lawson, R., & Waller, G. (2004). Compulsive features in the eating disorders: A role for trauma? *Journal of Nervous & Mental Disease, 192,* 247-249.

Mann, T., Tomiyama, A. J., Westling, E., Lew, A., Samuels, B., Chatman, J. (2007). Medicare's search for effective obesity treatments: Diets are not the answer. *American Psychologist, 62*(3), 220-233.

Mantero, M. & Crippa, L. (2002). Eating disorders and chronic post-traumatic stress disorder: Issues of psychopathology and comorbidity. *European Eating Disorders Review, 10,* 1-16.

O'Kearney, R. (1996). Attachment disruption in anorexia nervosa and bulimia nervosa: A review of theory and empirical research. *International Journal of Eating Disorders, 20*(2), 115-127.

Polivy, J. & Herman, P. (1985). Dieting and binging: A causal analysis. *American Psychologist, 40*(2), 193-201.

Polilvy, J. & Herman, P. (2002). Causes of eating disorders. *Annual Review of Psychology, 53,* 187-213.

Schore, A. N. (2000). Attachment and the regulation of the right brain. *Attachment & Human Development, 2*(1), 23-47.

Schore, A. N. (2002), Dysregulation of the right brain: a fundamental mechanism of traumatic attachment and the psychopathogenesis of posttraumatic stress disorder. *Australian and New Zealand Journal of Psychiatry, 36,* 9–30.

Ward, A., Ramsay, R. and Treasure, J. (2000), Attachment research in eating disorders. British Journal of Medical Psychology, 73: 35–51.

The U.S. Weight Loss Market: 2014 Status Report & Forecast. https://www.bharatbook.com/healthcare-market-research-reports/the-us-weight-loss-market-2014-status-report-forecast.html

Chapter 2

Arcelus J, Mitchell AJ, Wales J, Nielsen S. (2011). Mortality Rates in Patients with Anorexia Nervosa and Other Eating Disorders: A Meta-analysis of 36 Studies. *Archives of General Psychiatry, 68*(7): 724-731.

Costin, C. (2011). *8 Keys to Recovery from an Eating Disorder: Effective Strategies for Therapeautic Practice and Personal Experience.* New York: W.W. Norton.

Steinhausen, H.C. & Weber, S. (2009). The outcome of bulimia nervosa: findings from one-quarter century of research. *American Journal of Psychiatry, (166)*12: 1331-1341.

Chapter 3

Craig, A.D. (2014). *How do you Feel? An Interoceptive Moment with your Biological Self.* Princeton, NJ: Princeton University Press.

Damasio, A. R. (2000). *The feeling of what happens: Body and emotion in the making of consciousness.* New York: Harcourt Brace.

Faris, PL, Eckert, ED, Kim, S-W, Meller, W.H., Pardo, J.V., Goodale, L., & Hartman, B.K. (2006). Evidence for a vagal pathophysiology for bulimia nervosa and the accompanying depressive symptoms. *Journal of Affective Disorders, 92*(1), 79-90.

Faris, P.L., Hofbauer, R.D., Daughters, R., VandenLangenberg, E., Iversen, L., Goodale, R.L., Eckert, E.D., & Hartman, B.K. (2009). De-Stabilization of the Positive Vago-Vagal Reflex in Bulimia Nervosa. *Physiology & Behavior, 94*(1), 136-153.

Fogel, A. (2009). *The Psychophysiology of Self Awareness: Rediscovering the Lost Art of Body Sense.* New York, NY: W.W. Norton & Company.

Kaye, W. (2008). Neurobiology of anorexia and bulimia Purdue ingestive behavior research center symposium influences on eating and body weight over the lifespan: children and adolescents. *Physiology & Behavior, 94*(1), 121-135.

LeDoux J.E. (2002). *Synaptic Self: How our Brains Become Who We Are.* New York: Viking.

Merwin, R.M., Zucker, N.L., Lacy, J.L., & Elliott, C.A. (2010). Interoceptive awareness in eating disorders: distinguishing lack of clarity from non-acceptance of internal experience. *Cognition and Emotion, 24*(5), 892-902.

Saxena, S. & Feusner, J.D. (2006). Toward a neurobiology of body dysmorphic disorder. *Primary Psychiatry, 13*(7), 41-48.

Zucker, N.L., Merwin, R.M., Bulik, C.M., Moskovich, A., Wildes, J.E., & Groh, J. (2013). Subjective experience of sensation in anorexia nervosa. *Behavior Research and Therapy, 51*, 256-265.

Chapter 4

Clark, A. (1999). An embodied cognitive science? *Trends in Cognitive Sciences, 3*, 345–351.

Craig, A. D. (2004). Human feelings: Why are some more aware than others? *Trends in Cognitive Neuroscience, 8*, 239-241.

Fogel, A. (2013). *Body Sense: The Science and Practice of Embodied Self-Awareness.* New York: NY: W.W. Norton.

Graf, P., & Schacter, D. L. (1985). Implicit and explicit memory for new associations in normal subjects and amnesic patients. *Journal of Experimental Psychology: Learning, Memory, and Cognition, 16*, 978-992.

Holzel, B. K., Carmody, J., Vangel, M., Congleton, C., Yerramsetti, S. M., Gard, T., & Lazar, S.W. (2011). Mindfulness practice leads to increases in regional brain gray matter density. *Psychiatry Research: Neuroimaging, 191*, 36-43.

Levine, P. (1997). *Waking the tiger: Healing trauma.* Berkeley, CA: North Atlantic Books.

Levine, P. (2010). *In An Unspoken Voice: How the Body Releases Trauma and Restores Goodness.* Berkeley, CA: North Atlantic Books.

Porges, S.W. (2011). *The Polyvagal Theory: Neurophysiological Foundations of Emotions, Attachment, Communication, Self-Regulation.* New York: W.W. Norton.

Porges, S.W. (2004). Neuroception: A subconscious system for detecting threat and safety. *Zero to Three: Bulletin of the National Center for Clinical Infant Programs, 24*(5), 9-24.

Sapolsky, Robert M. *Why Zebras Don't Get Ulcers: A Guide to Stress, Stress Related Diseases, and Coping.* New York: W.H. Freeman.

Schubert, T. W., & Semin, G. (2009). Embodiment as a unifying perspective in psychology. *European Journal of Social Psychology, 39,* 1135–1141.

Squire, L. R. (2004). Memory systems of the brain: A brief history and current perspective. *Neurobiology of learning and memory, 82,* 171-177.

Wilson, M. (2002). Six views of embodied cognition. *Psychonomic Bulletin and Review, 9,* 625–636.

Chapter 5

Baldo, B. A., & Kelley, A. E. (2007). Discrete neurochemical coding of distinguishable motivational processes: Insights from nucleus accumbens control of feeding. *Psychopharmacology 191,* 439 – 459.

Balleine, B.W. (2005). Neural bases of food-seeking: affect, arousal and reward in Corticostriatolimbic circuits. *Physiology & Behavior, 86*(5):717–30.

Berthoid, H.R. (2008). Vagal and hormonal gut–brain communication: from satiation to satisfaction. *Neurogastroenterology & Motility, 20*(1): 64-72.

Jones, L.M., Fontanini, A. et al. (2006). Gustatory processing: a dynamic systems approach. *Current Opinion in Neurobiology, 16*(4):420–8.

Faris, P., Hofbauer, R. et al. (2008). Destabilization of the positive vago-vagal réflex in bulimia nervosa. *Physiology & Behavior, 94*(1), 136-153.

Van Oudenhove, L. et al. (2011). Fatty acid-induced gut-brain signaling attenuates neural and behavioral effects of sad emotions in humans. *Journal of Clinical Investigation, 121*(8): 3094-3099.

Chapter 6

Anderson, LK, Murray, SB, Ramirez, AL, Rockwell, R, LeGrange D, Kaye, WH. (2015). The integration of family-based treatment and dialectical behavior therapy for adolescents with bulimia nervosa: philosophical and practical considerations. *Eating Disorders: The Journal of Treatment & Prevention, 23*(4):325-35.

Chen, E.Y., Matthews, L., Allen, C., Kuo, J.R., Linehan, M.M. Dialectical behavior therapy for clients with binge-eating disorder or bulimia nervosa and borderline personality disorder. *International Journal of Eating Disorders, 41*(6): 505-12.

Kroger, C., Schweiger, U., Sipos, V., Kliem, S., Arnold, R., Schunert, T., Reinecker, H. (2010). Dialectical behaviour therapy and an added cognitive behavioural treatment module for eating disorders in women with borderline personality disorder and anorexia nervosa or bulimia nervosa who failed to respond to previous treatments. An open trial with a 15-month follow-up. *Journal of Behavior Therapy and Experimental Psychiatry, 41*(4):381-8.

Murray, S.B., Anderson, L.K., Cusack, A., Nakamura, T., Rockwell, R., Griffith, S., Kaye, W.H. Integrating Family-Based Treatment and Dialectical Behavior Therapy for Adolescent Bulimia Nervosa: Preliminary Outcomes of an Open Pilot Trial. *Eating Disorders: The Journal of Treatment & Prevention, 23*(4):336-44.

Safer, D.L., Telch, C.F., Chen, E. Y., & Linehan, M.M. (2009). *Dialectical Behavior Therapy for Binge Eating and Bulimia.* New York, NY: The Guilford Press.

Safer, D.L. & Tech, C.F. (2009). *Dialectical behavior therapy for binge eating and bulimia.* New York: The Guilford Press.

Safer, D. L., Telch, C. F. and Agras, W. S. (2001). Dialectical behavior therapy adapted for bulimia: A case report. *International Journal of Eating Disorders, 30*: 101–106.

Safer, D. L., Robinson, A. H., & Jo, B. (2010). Outcome From a Randomized Controlled Trial of Group Therapy for Binge Eating Disorder: Comparing Dialectical Behavior Therapy Adapted for

Binge Eating to an Active Comparison Group Therapy. *Behavior Therapy, 41*(1), 106–120.

Taitz, J. (2012). *End emotional eating: Using dialectical behavior therapy skills to cope with difficult emotions and develop a healthy relationship to food.* Oakland, CA: New Harbinger Publications.

Telch, C.F., Agras, W.S., & Linehan, M.M. (2001) Dialectical behavior therapy for binge eating disorder. *Journal of Consulting and Clinical Psychology, 69*(6), 1061-1065.

Wallace, L. M., Masson, P. C., Safer, D. L., & von Ranson, K. M. (2014). Change in emotion regulation during the course of treatment predicts binge abstinence in guided self-help dialectical behavior therapy for binge eating disorder. *Journal of Eating Disorders, 2*, 35.

Chapter 7

Brown, RP, Muench F, Gerbarg, PL. (2013). Breathing practices for treatment of psychiatric and stress-related medical conditions. In Complementary and Integrative Therapies for Psychiatric Disorders, Ed. *Psychiatric Clinics o North America, 36*(1):121-140.

Diamond, L. M., Fagundes, C. P., Butterworth, M. R. (2012). Attachment style, vagal tone, and empathy during mother–adolescent interactions". *Journal of Research on Adolescence,* 22 (1): 165–184.

Porges SW. (1992). Vagal Tone: A physiological marker of stress vulnerability. *Pediatrics, 90*:498-504.

Porges SW. (2001). The Polyvagal Theory: Phylogenetic substrates of a social nervous system. *International Journal of Psychophysiology 42*:123-146.

Porges SW. (2004). Neuroception: A subconscious system for detecting threat and safety. *Zero to Three: Bulletin of the National Center for Clinical Infant Programs, 24*:5,19-24.

Streeter CC1, Gerbarg PL, Saper RB, Ciraulo DA, Brown RP. (2012). Effects of yoga on the autonomic nervous system, gamma-aminobutyric-acid, and allostasis in epilepsy, depression, and post-traumatic stress disorder. *Medical Hypotheses, 78*(5): 571-9.

Thayer, J. F., & Sternberg, E. (2006). Beyond heart rate variability. *Annals of the New York Academy of Sciences, 1088*(1), 361-372.

Thayer, J. F., Åhs, F., Fredrikson, M., Sollers III, J. J., & Wager, T. D. (2012). A meta-analysis of heart rate variability and neuroimaging studies: implications for heart rate variability as a marker of stress and health. *Neuroscience & Biobehavioral Reviews, 36*(2), 747-756.

Thayer, J. F., Hansen, A. L., Saus-Rose, E., & Johnsen, B. H. (2009). Heart rate variability, prefrontal neural function, and cognitive performance: the neurovisceral integration perspective on self-regulation, adaptation, and health. *Annals of Behavioral Medicine, 37*(2), 141-153.

Villemure C, Čeko M, Cotton VA and Bushnell MC (2015) Neuroprotective effects of yoga practice: age-, experience-, and frequency-dependent plasticity. *Frontiers in Human Neurosci*ence 9:281. doi: 10.3389/fnhum.2015.00281

Williamson JB, Heilman KM, Porges EC, Lamb DG, Porges SW (2013). Possible mechanism for PTSD symptoms in patients with traumatic brain injury: central autonomic network disruption. *Frontiers in Neuroengineering.* doi: 10.3389/fneng

Nowakowski, M. E., McFarlane, T., & Cassin, S. (2013). Alexithymia and eating disorders: a critical review of the literature. *Journal of Eating Disorders,1,* 21.

References – Chapter 8

Craig AD. (2003) Interoception: The sense of the physiological condition of the body. *Current Opinions in Neurobiology, 13*(4)*:*500–505.

Craig, A.D. (2009). How do you feel – now? The anterior insula and human awareness. Nature Reviews Neuroscience *10*(1), 59-70.

Craig, A.D. (2015). *How do you feel? An interoceptive moment with your neurobiological self.* Princeton, NJ: Princeton University Press.

Damasio, A. (2000). *The Feeling of What Happens: Body and Emotion in the Making of Consciousness.* New York, NY: Mariner Books.

Damasio, A. (2010). *Self comes to mind: Constructing the conscious brain.* New York, NY: Knopf Doubleday Publishing Group.

Farb,N.A.S.,Segal,Z.V., & Anderson,A.K.(2013). Mindfulness meditation training alters cortical representations of interoceptive attention. *Social, Cognitive and Affective Neuroscience, 8*,15–26.

Herbert *et al.* (2012). Interoception across modalities: On the Relationship between Cardiac Awareness and the Sensitivity for Gastric Functions. *PLoS ONE.*

Herbert *et al.* (2013). Intuitive eating is associated with interoceptive sensitivity. Effects on body mass index. *Appetite.* doi: 10.1016/j.appet.2013.06.082

Holzel,B.K.,Carmody,J.,Vangel,M.,Congleton,C.,Yerramsetti,S.M.,Gard,T.,et al.(2011b). Mindfulness practice leads to increases in regional brain gray matter density. *Psychiatry Research, 191*, 36–43.

Levine, P.A., & Frederick, A. (1997). *Waking the Tiger: Healing Trauma.* Berkeley, CA: North Atlantic Books.

Levine, P.A. (2010). *In An Unspoken Voice: How the Body Releases Trauma and Restores Goodness.* Berkeley, CA: North Atlantic Books.

Nowakowski ME, McFarlane T, & Cassin S. (2013) Alexithymia and eating disorders: a critical review of the literature. *Journal of Eating Disorders, 1*(21).

Pollatos *et al.* (2008). Reduced perception of bodily signals in anorexia nervosa. *Eating Behaviors.* doi: 10.1016/j.eatbeh.2008.02.001

Porges, S.W. (2009). The polyvagal theory: New insights into adaptive reactions of the autonomic nervous system. *Cleveland Clinic Journal of Medicine, 76*(3):S86-S90

Porges, S.W. (2007). The polyvagal perspective. *Biological Psychology, Special Issue of Biological Psychology on Cardiac Vagal Control, Emotion, Psychopathology, and Health, 74*(2), 116-143.

Porges S.W. (2009). Reciprocal influences between body and brain in the perception and expression of affect: A polyvagal perspective. In

D Fosha, D Siegel, and M Solomon, eds. *The Healing Power of Emotion: Affective Neuroscience, Development, and Clinical Practice.* New York: Norton, 27-54.

Porges S.W. (2001). The Polyvagal Theory: Phylogenetic substrates of a social nervous system. *International Journal of Psychophysiology, 42*:123–146.

Chapter 9

Ainley V, Tsakiris M (2013). Body Conscious? Interoceptive Awareness, Measured by Heartbeat Perception, Is Negatively Correlated with Self Objectification. *PLoS ONE 8*(2): e55568. doi:10.1371/journal.pone.0055568

Brewer R, Cook R, Cardi V, Treasure J, Bird G. (2015). Emotion recognition deficits in eating disorders are explained by co-occurring alexithymia. *Royal Society Open Science, 2*: 140382. http://dx.doi.org/10.1098/rsos.140382

Carano A et al. (2006) Alexithymia and body image in adult outpatients with binge eating disorder. *International Journal of Eating Disorders,* 39, 332–340.

Chassler, L. (1997). Understanding anorexia nervosa and bulimia nervosa from an attachment perspective. *Clinical Social Work Journal, 25*(4), 407-423.

Cochrane, C., Brewerton, T., Wilson, D., Hodges, E. (1993). Alexithymia in the eating disorders. *International Journal of Eating Disorders, 14:* 219–222.

Cozolino, L. (2006). *The neuroscience of human relationships: Attachment and the developing brain.* New York: W.W. Norton & Co.

Fosha, D., Siegel, D., Solomon, M. (2009). *The Healing Power of Emotion: Affective Neuroscience, Development & Clinical Practice.* New York, NY: W.W. Norton.

Hund, A. & Espelage, D.L. (2006). Childhood emotional abuse and disordered eating among undergraduate females: Mediating influence of alexithymia, distress, and dissociation. *Child Abuse & Neglect, 30,* 393-407.

Marsero S, Ruggiero GM, Scarone S, Bertelli S, Sassaroli S. (2011). The relationship between alexithymia and maladaptive perfectionism in eating disorders: a mediation moderation analysis methodology. *Eating and Weight Disorders.* DOI: 10.1007/BF03325130

Pinaquy, S., Chabrol, H., Simon, C., Louvet, J.-P. and Barbe, P. (2003), Emotional Eating, Alexithymia, and Binge-Eating Disorder in Obese Women. *Obesity Research,* 11: 195–201. doi: 10.1038/oby.2003.31

Schmidt, U., Jiwany, A. & Treasure, J. (1993). A controlled study of alexithymia in eating disorders. *Comprehensive Psychiatry, 34*(1), 54-58.

Troop, N. A., Allan, S., Serpell, L. and Treasure, J. L. (2008), Shame in women with a history of eating disorders. *European Eating Disorders Review,* 16: 480–488.

Chapter 10

Albers, S. (2009). *Eat, Drink and Be Mindful.* Oakland, CA: New Harbinger Publications.

Bulik, C. (2015). *Crave: Why You Binge Eat and How to Stop.* New York, NY: Walker & Company.

Chozen Bays, J. (2009). *Mindful Eating: A Guide to Rediscovering a Healthy and Joyful Relationship to Food.* Boston & London: Shambala Publications.

Ginsburg, L. (2002). *What are you Hungry for? Women, Food, and Spirituality.* New York, NY: St. Martin's Griffin.

Herbert et al. (2011). Effects of short-term food deprivation on interoceptive awareness, feelings and autonomic cardiac activity. *Biological Psychology, 89*(1): 71-79

Herbert *et al.* (2012). Interoception across modalities: On the relationship between cardiac awareness and the sensitivity for gastric functions. *PLoS ONE.*

Herbert *et al.* (2013). Intuitive eating is associated with interoceptive sensitivity. Effects on body mass index. *Appetite.* doi: 10.1016/j.appet.2013.06.082

Jamieson, A. (2015). *Women, Food and Desire: Embrace your Cravings, Make Peace with Food, Reclaim your Body.* New York, NY: Gallery Books.

Marsh, S. (2015). *Hunger, Hope & Healing: A Yoga Approach to Reclaiming Your Relationship to Your Body and Food.* Boston & London: Shambala Publications.

May, M. (2011). *Eat What You Like, Like What you Eat: How to Break Your Eat-Repent-Repeat Cycle.* Publisher: Am I Hungry?

Pollatos *et al.* (2008). Reduced perception of bodily signals in anorexia nervosa. *Eating Behaviors, 9*(4):381-8

Roth, G. (2011). *Women, Food & God.* New York, NY: Scribner.

Tribole, E. & Resch, E. (2012). *Intuitive Eating.* New York, NY: St. Martin's Griffin.

Chapter 11

Goldstein, J. & Kornield, J. (2001). *Seeking the Heart of Wisdom: The Path of Insight Meditation.* Boston, MA: Shambala Classics.

Goldstein, J. (2003). *Insight Meditation: The Practice of Freedom.* Boston, MA: Shambala Classics.

Jung, C.G. (1999). *The Psychology of Kundalini Yoga.* Princeton, NJ: Princeton University Press.

Lipton, B. (2008). *The Biology of Belief: Unleashing the Power of Consciousness, Matter, & Miracles.* Carlsbad, CA: Hay House.

Parker Harris, J. (2000). *Jung and Yoga: The Psyche-Body Connection.* Toronto, Canada: Inner City Books.

Sandoz, E.K., Wilson, K.G., DuFrene, T. (2015). *Acceptance and Commitment Therapy for Eating Disorders: A Process-Focused Guide to Treating Anorexia and Bulimia.* New York, NY: New Harbinger Publications.

Stryker, R. (2011). *The Four Desires: Creating a Life of Purpose, Happiness, Prosperity, and Freedom.* New York, NY: Delacorte Press.

Tigunait, P.R. (2001). *At the Eleventh Hour: The Biography of Swami Rama.* Honesdale, PA: Himalayan Institute Press.

Chapter 12

Brown, B. (2010). *The Gifts of Imperfection: Let Go of Who You Think You're Supposed to Be and Embrace Who You Are.* Center City, MN: Hazelden Publishing.

Brown, B. (2013). *The Power of Vulnerability: Teachings on Authenticity, Connection and Courage.* Boulder, CO: Sounds True.

Kempton, S. (2013). *Awakening Shakti: The Transformative Power of the Goddesses of Yoga.* Boulder, CO: Sounds True.

Stryker, R. (2011). *The Four Desires: Creating a Life of Purpose, Happiness, Prosperity, and Freedom.* New York, NY: Delacorte Press.

Tigunait, P.R. (2007). *Tantra Unveiled: Seducing the Forces of Matter and Spirit.* Honesdale, PA: Himalayan Institute Press.

Resources

Academy of Eating Disorders (AED) – http://www.aedweb.org

Eating, Attachment & Somatic Education (EASE) – http://www.ease4eds.com

Eating Disorders Anonymous – http://www.eatingdisordersanonymous.org

Eating Disorder Coalition for Research, Policy and Action – http://www.eatingdisordercoalition.org

Eating Disorder Hope – http://www.eatingdisorderhope.com

Eating Disorders Information Network – http://www.myedin.org

Eating Disorder Referral (EDReferral) – http://www.edreferral.com

International Association of Eating Disorder Professionals (iaedp) – http://www.iaedp.com

Light of the Moon Café - http://www.lightofthemooncafe.com

Multi-Service Eating Disorder Association – http://www.medainc.org

National Association of Anorexia Nervosa and Associated Disorders – http://www.anad.org

National Eating Disorder Association – http://www.nationaleatingdisorders.org/

Somatic Experiencing Trauma Institute – http://www.traumahealing.com

Something Fishy – http://www.somethingfishy.org

Made in the USA
Middletown, DE
24 November 2015